AMERICA
IN VIETNAM

Text and Captions
Dr. John F. Guilmartin

Photography
UPI/Bettmann
National Archives, Washington, D.C.

Design
Sally Strugnell

Commissioning Editor
Andrew Preston

Commissioning Assistant
Edward Doling

Editorial
Gill Waugh

Production
Ruth Arthur
Sally Connolly
David Proffit
Andrew Whitelaw

Director of Production
Gerald Hughes

Director of Publishing
David Gibbon

AMERICA IN VIETNAM
THE FIFTEEN-YEAR WAR

DR. JOHN GUILMARTIN

Illustrations selected from the files of
UNITED PRESS INTERNATIONAL/BETTMANN

MILITARY PRESS

CONTENTS

INTRODUCTION
THE FIFTEEN-YEAR WAR

Quang Ngai villagers make their way through flooded paddies in November 1964: the monsoon rains have dictated the rhythms of Vietnamese life since time immemorial.

The Vietnam War, or simply Vietnam: how often do we hear the expression used offhandedly, in the unspoken belief that speaker and listener both understand what is meant? This assumption of shared understanding is deceptive, for the expression has become a code word for events, situations and conditions which, although related, are anything but synonymous. Depending on who says it and to whom, it can have strikingly different meanings, even historically. For the French, the primary reference is to the struggle between French colonial forces and the Viet Minh for control of Indochina, a

struggle which began in the wake of World War II and ended with the partition of Vietnam at Geneva in 1954. To the Vietnamese the phrase is evocative of a longer struggle, that for Vietnamese independence from foreign domination and colonial exploitation and for freedom from internal repression, though repression by whom depends on the speaker's political persuasion. The Vietnamese, communist and anti-communist alike, are likely to agree that the struggle began long ago and remains unresolved. Cambodians and Laotians view the war differently; though Cambodia and Laos, like

Left: peasants transfer water into a paddy with rope-and-bucket pumps. Although photographed in 1923, the scene depicted is timeless and would have looked the same as much as a thousand years ago.

Right: children at work weeding and transplanting seedlings in a rice paddy, October 1957. The annual cycle of rice cultivation has dominated Vietnamese village life from earliest times.

Hill 875, under attack by U.S. forces and shrouded in artillery smoke, 22 November, 1967. Beyond the coastal strip, much of South Vietnam is an unrelieved expanse of heavily jungled hills and valleys.

Vietnam, were part of the French Empire the three nations were swallowed up in the war at different times and in different ways. For Cambodia, the war entered a new phase when the Vietnamese invaded in December 1978 to overthrow the Khymer Rouge regime, a phase which still continues in a brutal, uncompromising and complex guerrilla war. China and the Soviet Union were also involved, and Chinese and Soviet perspectives on when the war started, when it ended – or if indeed it has – are no doubt both distinct and different from each other. The same point can be made with respect to the Thais, who were involved in support of the United States no less than were the Soviets and Chinese in support of Ho Chi Minh and his followers. America, of course, has its own perspective.

One might argue that the conflict should more properly be called the Southeast Asia War, as indeed it is on occasion, for it directly involved not just Vietnam, but also Laos, Cambodia, Thailand and, to a lesser extent, the Philippines, Australia and New Zealand. The other nations of Southeast Asia were indirectly involved in one way or another and, in many cases, this indirect involvement was pivotal: the modest Filipino commitment to South Vietnam in terms of civic actions and medical assistance pales in importance beside U.S. reliance on air and naval bases in the Philippines. U.S. bases in Taiwan and Japan, technically not Southeast Asian nations but nevertheless major economic powers in the region, were of comparable importance. The extent of direct Chinese involvement is a matter of debate: some analysts believe that construction troops and perhaps radar and anti-aircraft artillery units of the Chinese Peoples Liberation Army served in North Vietnam during the American phase of the war, and French sources assert that Chinese troops suppressed anti-communist guerrillas in northern North Vietnam. Be that as it may, the crucial importance of Chinese support to the Viet Minh, and later North Vietnam, both logistical and in terms of sanctuary provided is undisputed.

Moreover, much of the war was fought beyond the boundaries of Vietnam. The war in Laos is a case in point. This encompassed a complex struggle between indigenous royalists, communists and neutralists; a Viet Minh invasion which turned into an occupation; a struggle between communist forces and indigenous guerrillas, supported first by France, then by the U.S. and Thailand; and, finally, and arguably the most important point in terms of effort expended, a bitterly contested campaign by U.S. air forces to restrict the flow of communist supplies into South Vietnam along the Ho Chi Minh trail. The campaign against communist supply lines in southern Laos, mounted largely from Thai bases, was connected only incidentally to the rest of the war in Laos and was, in fact, part of the war in Vietnam in every way except geographically. The war spilled over into Thailand

French troops slog through an irrigation canal in the summer of 1953. Throughout Vietnam's history, the monsoon rains have dominated war as well as agriculture.

in the form of a communist-led insurgency in the northeast which was supported by North Vietnam. The southern termini of the Ho Chi Minh Trail were in Cambodia, and communist bases along the Cambodian/Vietnamese border featured prominently in the war from beginning to end. The Cambodian civil war which erupted after the Lon Nol coup of March 1970, though politically distinct from the struggles around it, was inseparable from them operationally, and the fall of Phnom Penh in April 1975 heralded that of Saigon less than two weeks later. The

struggle for popular support in the United States was also a decisive campaign of the war, one that was connected not only to events in Vietnam, but to the other struggles mentioned above. Significantly, anti-war activism in the United States peaked in the wake of President Nixon's invasion of Cambodia in the spring of 1970.

The conflict might even be considered global, with the Korean War constituting the first phase. In fact, the connections between Korea and Vietnam were many:

Vietnam. Free-world shipping clogged Saigon harbor and, during the American phase, Haiphong harbor was similarly clogged with ships of the Warsaw Pact nations. At one time or another, Indian, Canadian, Polish and Hungarian troops saw peace-keeping duty in Indochina, and Cuban interrogators were given access to captured American aviators in North Vietnam.

However, in the final analysis, Vietnamese considerations predominated. The major strategic issues of the war were resolved by the hostilities which began in 1946 near Haiphong, impelled by the Vietnamese desire for independence from French rule, and ended in 1975 with the fall of Saigon to the Peoples Army of Vietnam (PAVN). The political factors that established the pace and geographic focus of the conflict were Vietnamese throughout and, when all is said and done, the outcome was determined by Vietnamese leaders and Vietnamese combatants. This is not to deny the importance of external intervention; the shape, pace and intensity of the war was determined at times by the French, the Chinese, the Americans and the Soviets. The Viet Minh victory at Dien Bien Phu would have been impossible without Chinese and Soviet logistic support, and the same point can be made with respect to the final communist offensive which took Saigon. Similarly, the armed forces of the Republic of Vietnam (ARVN) would not have fought as long and hard as they did without massive U.S. logistic and technical assistance. Nevertheless, the center of gravity of the war was Vietnamese from beginning to end and that is why the term Vietnam War fits ... not perfectly, perhaps, but then few such labels do.

To approach the conflict from the American viewpoint does not imply value judgement, simply fact. The United States of America became deeply involved in Vietnam and that involvement had serious consequences. That those consequences affected not only America – nor even particularly America – renders the American perspective no less valid. The impact of the war on the nations of Southeast Asia – Vietnam, Laos and Cambodia in particular – was far greater, a point too many Americans are prone to forget. But that impact was shaped in no small measure by the United States, its armed forces and its government. Finally, the United States which emerged from Vietnam was very different from the one which went in, a matter of no small significance in international affairs. Thus, even if we accept the primacy of the Asian point of view, the American perspective is still worth examining in its own right. This book concentrates on the period from 1960, the middle of a period of transition between the Eisenhower and Kennedy administrations, in which the preservation of a non-communist South Vietnam became a national policy underwritten by military action, and 1975, when the fall of Saigon marked the failure of that policy.

A lightly wounded Marine holds his injured arm; he's one of the fortunate – for the moment. The threat of death and injury is the soldier's constant companion.

French forces fought in Korea and communist China supplied the Viet Minh with U.S. equipment captured there; later, South Korea dispatched a major expeditionary force to South Vietnam. American aviators over North Vietnam and Laos fought against more advanced versions of the Soviet air defense systems which had opposed them in Korea and Soviet sources have recently confirmed that Soviet troops, notably surface-to-air missile (SAM) specialists, saw combat in

CHAPTER ONE

1850 1945 BACKGROUND TO ARMAGEDDON

A father and son go about their business in Cholon in the aftermath of the communist "Little Tet" attacks, May 1968. Throughout the war, the Vietnamese did their best to lead normal lives.

During the years of U.S. military involvement in Vietnam, American newscasters and editorialists often described that country as small and far away. There were elements of truth in this characterization but, as with most clichés, it was chosen for aptness rather than accuracy and must be qualified. With regard to distance, a look at the globe shows that Saigon, now Ho Chi Minh City, and Hanoi are almost exactly opposite New York in longitude, about as far apart as it is possible for places to be in the northern hemisphere. But America is a big country, and the distance from New York to San Francisco is nearly a fourth that from New York to Saigon. Vietnam, moreover, is separated from North America mainly by ocean, and the broad expanses of the Pacific have presented few impediments to navigation since the advent of transoceanic steamships in the second half of the nineteenth century. Intercontinental air travel, a practical

reality since the late 1930s, shrank the distance further still. During World War II, the United States maintained a regular air service across the Pacific from California to Australia and, over even greater distances, from Florida to China by way of South America, Africa and India. That Vietnam was omitted almost entirely from America's wartime calculations was due to political and strategic imperatives, and not to distance. When, in the waning years of French colonial rule, Vietnam dawned on the American consciousness, there were many parts of the world more inaccessible to America in terms of time and expense. The question of size is also relative. Vietnam is small compared to the United States, but size alone means little. As strategic analyst Harry Summers has noted, Vietnam is only slightly smaller than the Germany which opposed America in two world wars.

Another familiar cliché in the years of dawning American awareness was that Vietnam was a new nation. In fact Vietnam was old, with a strong, coherent culture and well-established traditions of independence, but most of what Americans knew about Vietnam came from the French, who downplayed the traditions of the nation they had subjugated. Lack of awareness of these realities was among the first of many American misperceptions of Vietnam which cost both countries dearly.

The first record of Vietnam is in Chinese documents of the early fifth century B.C. which refer to a Viet kingdom south of the Yangtze River. By the mid-fourth century B.C., the Viet kingdom had fallen and its populace, along with other non-Han groups in what is today southern China, notably the Thai, Lao and Hmong, migrated south in response to Chinese pressure. About 207 B.C., Vietnamese polities from the area west of present-day Canton to the Red River Delta and as far south as modern Hue united as Nam, or southern, Viet. Vietnamese civilization had by then assumed its essential character, marked by the wet cultivation of rice, capable of sustaining much higher population densities than

At a landing zone near Phuc Vinh, June 1967, a GI (right) of the 1st Infantry Division contends with the demands of the war and the monsoon rains as best he can.

Viet Cong bodies laid out for inspection by U.S. advisors, November 1964. Death is an inevitable product of war, but it was given a peculiarly inhuman aspect by Secretary of Defense Robert McNamara's emphasis on body count.

competing methods of food production, notably upland farming based on slash and burn methods, and the organization of social and economic activity in family, village and clan units.

Indochina is separated from China by a heavily jungled, mountainous region of incredible ruggedness and striking beauty, not readily penetrated by commerce; this was to form an effective barrier to southward Chinese population movement, though not to cultural and political influence. The main points of entry from the north are through a handful of mountain passes and the Red River valley. Geographically, eastern Indochina is dominated by the Annamite mountain chain, the Red River and the Mekong River, all running generally northwest to southeast. The Annamite chain separates the valleys of the Red and the Mekong rivers and follows the modern Vietnamese/Laotian border to a point some fifty miles north of Saigon with heavily forested peaks ranging in height from 5,000 feet to 8,500 feet; the chain is penetrated by a limited number of east/west passes, notably Barthelemy pass, linking the coastal plain to the Plaine des Jarres in Laos, and Nape and Mhu Gia passes linking the coastal plain to the middle Mekong.

The Red River rises in southwestern Yunnan and flows southeast, broadening into a delta which forms the demographic and political heart of northern Vietnam. The Mekong originates in the Himalayas, flows south through Yunnan into northern Laos, and delineates the present Thai/Laotian boundary before running back into Laos; it then bisects Cambodia before entering Vietnam southeast of Saigon and spreading out into a broad delta. By the logic of culture and geography, the middle Mekong should be the heart of a Lao nation encompassing most of what is today northwestern Thailand, and so indeed it was from the mid-fifteenth century to the late seventeenth. But civil war weakened the country and Laos was in the process of absorption by Thailand when French annexation in 1893 fixed the border at the Mekong. Similarly, the lower Mekong and its delta should be the heart of the Khymer nation and once were, but, as with Laos, French annexation in 1863 prevented the absorption of Cambodia by its neighbors. There was, however, an important difference: while the Thai and the Lao are closely related, with mutually intelligible languages, the Khymer are culturally and linguistically distinct from the other peoples of Indochina. In the ninth and tenth centuries, Khymer kings ruled most of Indochina west of the Annamites from their capital at Angkor Wat, but the kingdom contracted under Thai and Vietnamese pressure and was in decline when Europeans reached Southeast Asia. But for French intervention, the Khymer would likely have been reduced to a dwindling population under Vietnamese and Thai rule; indeed, the Mekong Delta, conquered by Vietnam in the late 1700s, still has a Khymer minority as do the border provinces of southeastern Thailand. The Mekong Delta, a highly fertile rice-growing region, dominates southeastern Indochina physically and economically much as the Red River Delta dominates the north.

Geography did much to shape the history of Vietnam. The Annamite chain channeled Vietnamese expansion, concentrating settlement in the Red River Delta and the narrow coastal plain; it also channeled the flow of ideas, determining that the main intellectual influence on Vietnam would be Chinese rather than Indian and that Bhuddism and Confucian forms of government would prevail. Geography and culture determined that the Vietnamese would occupy the small portion of the land suitable for paddy rice cultivation, outnumbering the aboriginal inhabitants and pushing them back into the highlands. The monsoon, the seasonal wind which flows steadily from the northwest in winter, then reverses during the summer, reinforced the influence of geography. During the winter, moist winds sweeping off the South China Sea and the Gulf of Tonkin back up against the mountains and turn to rain, providing the rice cultivators of the Red River Delta and the coastal plain with a reliable source of water for irrigation. The summer monsoon brings rain to the west of the mountains and clear weather to the east. The predictability of the monsoon and its rains is central to the Vietnamese way of life and to the military history of Vietnam, for military forces move with difficulty, if at all, during the wet monsoon.

An M-60 gunner writes home in a rare moment of rest, mid-January 1968. Separation from loved ones can prey on a soldier's mind.

The Han dynasty overthrew the Viet kingdom in 111 B.C., and from then until A.D. 938, when the Vietnamese expelled their foreign overlords, Vietnam was part of the Chinese empire. Vietnam did not take kindly to Chinese rule, and the period was punctuated with rebellions, including one during 43-39 B.C. led by two sisters, Trung Trac and Trung Nhi, who, according to legend, drowned themselves rather than admit defeat. Two centuries later another female revolutionary leader, Trieu An, followed the Trungs' example by committing suicide after a failed rebellion. All three are considered national heroines. Though details are scant, the Vietnamese struggle for independence was bitter. Scholars generally accept the idea that the Reconquista, the seven centuries of struggle by which Iberian Christians threw off Muslim rule, left an indelible mark on the history of Spain and Portugal. It should be no surprise that the equivalent Vietnamese struggle, which lasted some three centuries longer, from, in European terms, the heyday of the Roman Republic through the founding of the Norman kingdom, and encompassing the entire history of Imperial Rome, left an equally strong imprint.

Vietnamese independence did not go unchallenged, nor was the internal history of Vietnam tranquil. Mongol invasions penetrated Vietnam three times, in 1247, 1284 and 1287, only to be repulsed. In 1407 the Mings, taking advantage of dynastic turmoil, reimposed Chinese rule only to be thrown out by a guerrilla rebellion twenty years later. A palace coup in 1527 led to civil war, and in 1673 a truce between the contending Trinh dynasty in the north and the Nguyen in the south divided the country at a point not far from the 17th parallel. The partition lasted until 1788, no doubt reinforcing north/ south cultural and linguistic differences. All the while Vietnam continued to expand southward, overwhelming the neighboring Champa civilization in the fifteenth century and waging a series of sharp, decisive wars with the Khymers late in the seventeenth which brought the Mekong Delta under Vietnamese control.

Indochina had little to offer Europeans, and the dominant peoples of Indochina – the Vietnamese, Thais and Burmese – were better able to defend themselves than most other Asians. In consequence, Burma and Vietnam fell under European control only at the end of the era of colonial expansion and Thailand remained free. The first European lodgement in Vietnam was a Portuguese trading station established in 1535 at Faifo, some fifteen miles south of modern Da Nang; it was to remain the only one for three centuries. The initial European impact was made by Catholic missionaries, notably Jesuits. Perhaps aided in their work by the turmoil of civil war, they were better received in Vietnam than in most other parts of Asia and made numerous converts, particularly in the southern Red River Delta, where they formed the only significant body of native

Christians on the Asian mainland.

Among the second generation of missionaries was one Alexandre de Rhodes, a French Jesuit who arrived under Portuguese auspices in 1627, became fluent in Vietnamese and developed the Latin *quoc ngu* script. Rhodes' alphabet, an intellectual achievement of the first order, was to help turn Vietnam culturally toward the west. Recognizing the decline of Portuguese power, Rhodes lobbied the Vatican to place Vietnam under French ecclesiastical auspices, which it did in 1664, constituting the first small step toward French domination.

Vietnam, Cambodia and Laos fell to France almost by default. France's strategic concerns focused on the continent of Europe, but whenever visionaries like Colbert, Louis XIV's brilliant naval minister, managed to erect the basis for a coherent colonial strategy, they were undercut by a change in regime. Direct involvement in Vietnam came in 1787 under Louis XVI with the consummation of a treaty, drawn up by a Jesuit missionary, to intervene in a Vietnamese civil war on behalf of an overthrown Nguyen dynast. The intervention succeeded despite the disapproval of its royal patron, who was overthrown by the Revolution before he could cancel the expedition; from the French perspective it accomplished little beyond securing a degree of toleration for Catholicism, which faded as apprehensions of European influence grew. After a false start in 1847 under Louis Philippe, the French gained a foothold in Vietnam in 1859 under Napoleon III, when a small

One Marine shaves his buddy's head while another scans Life *magazine for news from home. In the combat zone, daily routines went on despite the apparent incongruity.*

Troopers of the U.S. 1st Air Cavalry Division search for the Viet Cong after using tear gas grenades to flush villagers from their bunkers. For civilians caught in the middle during a war, fear is never absent for long.

garrison, put into Saigon as an afterthought to a punitive expedition prompted by persecution of missionaries and local Catholics, seized Da Nang as a means of forcing the Emperor to make Vietnam a French protectorate. The incident ended instead in humiliating withdrawal, leaving the Saigon garrison isolated until it was relieved two years later. Using Saigon for leverage, the French coerced the Emperor progressively to cede control over adjacent provinces, and by 1867 France controlled all of southern Vietnam, renamed Cochinchina.

From this beginning, French control expanded more in response to local impulse and opportunity than in pursuit of any grand design. Fear of losing out to another European power in the game of colonial expansion counted for more than rational economic calculation,

U.S. troops were not the only foreign soldiers in Vietnam during America's fifteen-year war. A terrified mother (right) shields her child as a South Korean soldier looks on, March 1966.

Left: a woman holds a wounded child near Dau Tieng, 20 March, 1975. Contentions that Asians value human life less than westerners ignore intense family bonds of loyalty and affection.

Cambodia, and completed it with the annexation of Laos in 1893.

A quiet interlude in the Imperial Citadel of Hue in the spring of 1972. Throughout Vietnam's long history, war has brought young men and women together only to force them to part again.

and the costs of conquest more than offset any economic gain. Not until the turn of century did the French make their empire self-supporting by means of a system of taxation and state-run monopolies, including salt and opium, which came down disproportionately on the indigenous populace. In 1874, the Emperor recognized Cochinchina as a French colony, in order to secure the withdrawal of a French force that had seized Hanoi on its own initiative. In 1879, the French reoccupied Hanoi and expanded their control over the Red River valley and contiguous provinces, which they dubbed Tonkin. When the boy emperor, Ham Nghi, protested, French marines attacked and looted the imperial palace at Hue; the Emperor fled, ordering a national uprising, only to be captured and exiled to Algeria. Replacing Ham Nghi with a compliant brother, the French tightened their control over Annam, as they termed central Vietnam, snuffing out the last vestiges of independence. France formalized her conquest in 1887 with the formation of the Indochinese Union, consisting of Tonkin, Annam, Cochinchina and

The Vietnamese took no more kindly to French rule than they had to Chinese, but modern weaponry and European military discipline rendered overt resistance futile. The expedition that took Hanoi in 1879 consisted of only two companies of infantry, or 600 men, and if considerably more troops were required to stifle opposition in the countryside – 20,000 were stationed in Tonkin by the end of 1883 – the military equation still favored the Europeans. It is worth noting, too, that the Vietnamese institutions which the French replaced had been showing signs of strain when the French appeared, and that opposition to the Nguyen dynasty, restored with French aid in 1802, had a strong anti-mandarin flavor. Opposition, while often bitter, was uncoordinated and lacked a popular base of support and, by the eve of World War I, resistance in the name of traditional values had effectively flickered out.

French control lasted less than seventy years, but it had a profound effect on Indochina, particularly Vietnam. The French banned Chinese pictographs and mandated the use of *quoc ngu* script, and, though the results hardly produced broad-based literacy, traditional Confucian respect for education diverted into Western channels. Educated Vietnamese, particularly those schooled in France, were exposed to liberal and radical political thought … and to the contrast between the ideals of Voltaire and Montesquieu and the condescending, racist arrogance of their colonial masters. Unsurprisingly, a high proportion of Vietnamese nationalists and revolutionary leaders were French educated.

Some few colonialists took their "civilizing mission" seriously, and in Cambodia and Laos the French were generally well received. The creation of roads, rail lines and basic health services benefited a portion of the populace. Though part of the blame must be laid on the French, the Vietnamese imperial government had been notably unsuccessful in maintaining public peace in its final years, particularly in Tonkin, and the imposition of order was no doubt an improvement in many areas. The French showed favor to the upland minorities, the Malayo-Polynesian Montagnards in the south and the more advanced T'ai, Hmong and other Sino-Tibetan hill tribes in the north†, who had been exploited or ignored under Vietnamese and Laotian rule. While the French hardly replaced ignorance and disorder with civilization, there were positive aspects to French rule. Southern Vietnam, in particular, was generally prosperous under the French, though this was mainly a product of the fertility of the Mekong Delta and the hard work of the peasantry.

The French in Indochina were not the worst of colonialists; indeed, if such a characterization can be made, they were arguably among the best. They could not match the Belgians in Africa for brutality, the Japanese in Manchuria and Korea for ruthlessness and racist arrogance nor the Dutch in Indonesia for naked commercial exploitation. They left behind in Indochina a reverence for their language, educational institutions, culture and cuisine which places them ahead of the Spanish in the Philippines, the Dutch in Indonesia and the British in Burma. If the French stand up poorly in comparison with the British in India – which might be contested – it was no doubt in part because Indochina was far less important to France than was India to Britain and in part because Britain's overseas policies had a degree of coherence and continuity imposed from above. Further, the enormity of Britain's strategic problems in India forced the British into power-sharing alliances with local elites, which both softened the edge of exploitation and made disassociation easier when it came. Tellingly, by the late nineteenth century, locally recruited units of the British Indian Army were officered largely by Indians whereas French colonial troops recruited from among the indigenous peoples of Indochina were commanded almost entirely by French officers and non-commissioned officers to the bitter end.

By and large, the French treated their Asian subjects to no greater economic and social outrages than did most other colonialists, and there is truth in the assertion that the French in Vietnam "belonged" in a way that Americans never did. Yet the Vietminh-led struggle against the French which erupted after World War II was marked by a peculiar intensity and bitterness, a bitterness which carried over into the American phase of the conflict. Why was this? The Vietnamese tradition of resistance to foreign domination was no doubt a major factor. Another reason which bears consideration was the sharp contrast between theory and practice in French colonialism; the French were no worse than most and a good deal better than many, but the contrast between the realities of colonial exploitation and the French ideals of law, justice and government – *liberté, fraternité, egalité* – was particularly stark. Could it be that Vietnamese nationalists felt not only abused, but in a sense betrayed?

The villager's view of the war in a single picture: a mother and her children swim to safety from their village near Qui Nhon, under U.S. air attack in September 1965.

CHAPTER TWO

THE FRENCH WAR

1945 54

The beginning of the end for France in Indochina: Japanese troops march into Haiphong in November 1940, to secure airfield and port facilities for use against the Chinese.

At the beginning of the twentieth century the position of the French in Indochina seemed secure. They maintained power with a combination of coercion and co-option which undermined the legitimacy of traditional values at the top. By imposing individual monetary taxes, they also undermined the collective importance of the village – the most basic of all Vietnamese institutions – and weakened the structure of Vietnamese society at the bottom. The strength of traditional values was further eroded by forced adoption of the *quoc ngu* alphabet and the obvious superiority of French scientific and technical education. Opposition to French rule had no clear issue around which to coalesce. The French were adept at playing on religious and ethnic differences to pit groups against one another; they also made effective use of local intermediaries to wield power, partly to deflect resentment away from the colonial regime and partly to co-opt indigenous elites. Control of the commercial economy, particularly that of Saigon and the all-important rice trade, was left largely in the hands of Chinese merchants. The French used the mandarin class to provide low-level functionaries; at the same time they supervised the details of government down to the lowest level by means of a swollen bureaucracy, employing nearly as many Europeans in Indochina as did the British in India to govern a populace barely a tenth as large. Characteristically, the French maintained the Nguyen emperors in Hue to preserve the appearance of legitimacy while reducing the imperial government to impotence.

Rebellion in the name of traditional Vietnamese values had flickered out by the beginning of World War I, the tradition of resistance to foreign lords overwhelmed by an alien culture and economic system imposed by unanswerable military might. Such rebellions as occurred were local in scope and were quickly put down by French troops aided by native auxiliaries.

But with the First World War, new standards of rebellion arose in the form of nationalism and socialism, more precisely revolutionary communism. When American President Woodrow Wilson proclaimed his Fourteen Points as a basis for ending the war, he included among them the principle of national self-determination. The diplomats at Versailles – and indeed Wilson himself – had no intention of applying the principle beyond Europe, but the cat was out of the bag. Wilson had given nationalism based on ethnic, linguistic and cultural affinity legitimacy among oppressed colonial peoples. At the same time, the success of the Bolshevik revolution had given credibility and prestige to the ideas of Karl Marx and made plausible the notion of an international revolution of the oppressed in the name of socialism. Communist theorists quickly identified colonialism as a form of capitalist exploitation, and national communist parties appeared throughout the

Above: the Haiphong docks on 9 August, 1942. Japanese targets in French Indochina came under attack from China-based U.S. aircraft. Vietnam was not, however, central to America's strategic interests in World War II.

Left: Japanese cargo vessels burn off the Vietnamese coast after being attacked by U.S. carrier aircraft in January 1945.

Ho Chi Minh, staunch Vietnamese patriot, brilliant leader and seasoned Marxist-Leninist revolutionary, pictured during negotiations with the French in 1946.

Summer 1950: a French soldier disarms a Vietminh during a seize-and-hold operation. French pacification efforts were highly successful during 1949 and 1950, but were later de-emphasized.

A French NCO and Cambodian partisans on patrol. French efforts to recruit non-Vietnamese troops for use against the Vietminh, though effective, were never pursued systematically.

23

colonial world. The Comintern, organized as the Communist International in 1919 by the Soviet Union to turn the ideal of revolution into reality, gave aid and guidance to the nascent communist parties.

The tension between nationalism and communism, evident in Vietnam from the beginning, reflected a broader contest as these two powerful strains of political thought struggled for the soul of Asia. By the early 1930s, active resistance to the French had appeared in Vietnam under both banners, notably in the form of the Viet Nam Quoc Dan Dang (VNQDD, Vietnamese Nationalist Party), inspired by the Chinese Kuomintang, and the nascent Vietnamese Communist party.

At this point, one of the most remarkable figures in history enters our narrative: Ho Chi Minh. Born Nguyen Sinh Cung on May 19, 1890, the son of an impoverished mandarin in Nghe Ahn province, he was infected at an early age with a deep desire to expel the French (one of the many aliases which he adopted over the years was Nguyen Ai Quoc, "Nguyen the Patriot"). Recognizing the futility of overt resistance, he left Vietnam as a sailor aboard a French ship in 1912 not to return for three decades. His wanderings as an itinerant revolutionary were the stuff of legend, improbably perfect in light of his chosen vocation. He spent a year in New York and later wrote a perceptive analysis of the Ku Klux Klan. He worked under renowned chef Georges Escoffier as a cook at London's Carlton Hotel, rising to assistant pastry chef, no mean gastronomic achievement. In Paris during the Versailles negotiations, he drafted a statement supporting Vietnamese national self-determination to hand President Wilson, only to be refused. In December of 1920 he was present at the birth of the French Communist Party as a founding member. As a Comintern agent, he founded the Indochina Communist Party in Hong Kong in 1930, shortly thereafter returning to Vietnam. In Moscow during the late 1930s, he survived Stalin's purges only to be imprisoned by Chiang Kai-shek during World War II.

Was Ho Chi Minh nationalist or communist? The easy answer, and probably the best, is that the question is irrelevant for he was both. His credentials as a nationalist are unimpeachable, yet he was unswerving in his adherence to the theory and practice of Marxist-Leninist revolution and stands in the legendary first generation of communist leaders alongside Lenin, Trotsky and Mao Tse-tung.

The communists at first concentrated on organization and on developing their theory, downplaying direct revolutionary action. Meanwhile the VNQDD was attacking French officials and assassinating collaborators, and many of Ho's colleagues urged a more active communist role. Ho's policy of restraint was vindicated when the French attacked the nationalists with brutal effectiveness in 1930-31 and the communists

A dapper Emperor Bao Dai, dressed in crepe-soled shoes and a sports jacket better suited to his Parisian haunts than the combat zone, reviews French-led Vietnamese paratroops inside the Hoa Binh perimeter, in December 1951. Behind him is General René Cogny.

Right: Vo Nguyen Giap reviews Vietminh troops in 1952. Although less imposing in terms of military decorum than the French, the Vietminh possessed impressive discipline and were also able and willing to learn from their mistakes.

Evidence of widening U.S. involvement in Vietnam, the escort carrier USS Windham Bay *(below), with a deckload of F8F Bearcat fighters, lies in Saigon docks in February 1951.*

moved against their rivals at an early stage by liquidating thousands of nationalists, at times with French connivance. Then, in 1939, a French crackdown forced Ho's cadres to go underground or flee.

At this low ebb in their fortunes the Communists were saved by World War II and, improbably, by Japanese imperialism. When Japan moved into Vietnam in 1940, France had fallen to Nazi Germany and Indochina was under the Vichy regime, nominally a Japanese ally. The Japanese quickly put down such resistance as the French offered, installed garrisons and took control of strategic airfields, but left the colonial regime in place. Then, in March of 1945, with Nazi Germany defeated and Japan's days numbered, partisans of French leader Charles de Gaulle attempted a coup. Their plans were compromised and the Japanese struck first, interning French troops, imprisoning their leaders and replacing them with a Vietnamese puppet government. For its leader they turned to the last of the Nguyen Emperors, French-educated Bao Dai, crowned as a boy in 1932.

Meanwhile, in May of 1941 Ho had organized the Viet Nam Doc Lap Dong Minh Hoi, the "League for the Independence of Vietnam", Vietminh for short. A well known communist as Nguyen Ai Quoc, he changed his name to Ho Chi Minh to conceal his party affiliation. Vietminh cadres set up base camps in the jungles of the Viet Bac, between the Red River Delta and the Chinese border, and began the patient work of organization, training and recruitment, working at first mainly among non-Vietnamese mountain tribes. During a trip to China in August of 1942, Ho fell into nationalist hands and was jailed, only to be released the following September and sent south with a monthly subsidy of 100,000 Chinese dollars to foment anti-Japanese resistance. The Vietminh contribution to the struggle against Japan was minimal, but they attracted the attention of the American OSS, receiving aid in the form of a team dropped in to coordinate efforts to assist downed U.S. aviators.

On 6 August, 1945, the first atomic bomb destroyed Hiroshima. Two days later a second destroyed Nagasaki and Japan surrendered within a week. In the preceding months, popular support for the Vietminh had increased dramatically, particularly in the north. Ho and his cadres concealed their communist identity and, with the French discredited and the Japanese defeated, stepped into the power vacuum, proclaiming themselves legitimate rulers of Vietnam. Bao Dai abdicated on 25 August, handing over his imperial seal to Ho Chi Minh. Ho Chi Minh proclaimed the Democratic Republic of Vietnam in Hanoi on 2 September, the same day that General Douglas MacArthur accepted Japan's surrender in Tokyo Bay.

From the standpoint of the victorious Allies, the situation in Indochina was ambiguous. Japan was in control and Washington and London viewed France's new leader, General De Gaulle, with suspicion. The Allies divided Indochina at the 16th parallel, and gave the responsibility for accepting the Japanese surrender to nationalist China in the north and to Britain in the south. The British landed a division of the Indian Army under Major General Douglas Gracey at Saigon. He found a Provisional Executive Committee, with a Vietminh minority, nominally in charge and anti-French sentiment running high. Responding to pleas from French inhabitants, Gracey released French troops from Japanese internment and ordered all Vietnamese disarmed. The nationalists responded by calling a general strike. Disorder spread and Gracey used rearmed French troops to help restore order. Cochinchina was plunged into civil war.

Anti-communist partisans move into the Red River Delta in January 1951. Although the French-sponsored Vietnamese National Army was a failure overall, its members often fought with both skill and determination.

Above: one of the ill-fated light commando battalions of the French-trained Vietnamese National Army, photographed in the field in late summer 1953.

In the north, the Vietminh retained control until the appearance of Chinese troops under General Lu Han in mid-September. With American acquiescence, the Chinese kept the interned French troops in detention and systematically looted the economy, manipulating the currency and seizing the Laotian opium crop. Meanwhile the Truman Administration recognized French sovereignty over Indochina, turning away from President Roosevelt's anti-colonialism. The French built up their forces in Saigon, and in October armored units under General Philippe Leclerc broke the Vietminh blockade and began a pacification campaign in the South.

Ho flew to France to negotiate the future of Vietnam, but France was unwilling to recognize independence in any meaningful form; not even the French Communists spoke up in his behalf. The ensuing maneuverings were complex, but the upshot was that Ho, bereft of international support and fearing prolonged Chinese occupation, invited the French back. By April, French troops had relieved the Chinese in Tonkin and were warily confronting the Vietminh in Hanoi and Haiphong. Negotiations ground on, but to no avail, and tensions increased as both sides prepared for war. What set off the spark is unclear: the Vietminh claimed it was the unwarranted seizure of a Vietnamese fishing vessel in Haiphong harbor on 20 November, 1946, while the French maintained the vessel was transporting arms. However that may be, fighting broke out. The French bombarded Haiphong with heavy loss of civilian life and on 19 December the Vietminh rose against the French. The Vietnam War had begun.

French forces quickly cleared the untrained Vietminh from Hanoi and Haiphong and by March they controlled

the cities, the major connecting arteries and most of the productive agricultural land of Vietnam, at least in daylight. In the north, the Vietminh retreated into the wilderness of the Bac Viet where, under the patient eyes of their cadres, they began the slow business of organizing and training for the struggle to come. The overconfident French failed to use the remaining two or three months of dry weather and in so doing missed perhaps their best – and last – chance of victory. With the return of the dry monsoon in October of 1947, the French took the offensive with a vengeance, dropping paratroops into the heart of Vietminh base areas in the Bac Viet. An armored column swept north along the Chinese border and then south from Cao Bang to link up with the paratroops, while a riverine force pressed up the Red River forming the second arm of a giant pincers. Ho and Giap were nearly captured as the paratroops found letters prepared for their signatures still on their desks. From there, things went downhill for the French. The Vietminh put up a dogged resistance, delaying the

The curtain rises on France's last act in Indochina: a French paratrooper (below) in action in the drop zone around Dien Bien Phu, on 20 November, 1953.

armored column and forcing the paratroops to fight unassisted for nine days. More importantly, the French failed to draw Giap's forces into a set-piece battle where they could be destroyed; it was the first of many such failures.

For two years, the French bided their time, staking out an outpost line along *Route Coloniale* 4 (RC 4) on the Chinese border, securing the allegiance of Tai tribes in the north, obtaining the cooperation of the Cao Dai and Hoa Hao religious sects in the south and engaging in more or less effective pacification operations in the Mekong and Red River deltas. They did not grant meaningful power to the anti-communist nationalists, but clung instead to Bao Dai. Manipulated by the Japanese and humiliated by Ho, Bao Dai was demoralized and corrupt, but made a compliant figurehead behind whom French administrators and commercial interests could pursue business as usual. Then, in December of 1949, Mao Tse-tung's victorious Chinese communists arrived at the border and the strategic equation changed dramatically. In the name of revolutionary solidarity, Mao provided the Vietminh with base camps in China and with American arms and equipment captured from the nationalists. The Vietminh built up their guerrilla cadres and trained and resupplied their main force units. In October of 1950 they struck, collapsing the outpost chain along RC 4 in the greatest French colonial defeat since the loss of Canada to Britain in 1763.

French panic was stopped by the arrival of General Jean de Lattre de Tassigny, a remarkable leader and arguably France's best general of the war. De Lattre cancelled an evacuation of French noncombatants from Tonkin, purged incompetent officers and inspired the rest; he began the construction of a series of defensive positions, the de Lattre Line, around the all-important Red River Delta, to free his mobile reserves for offensive operations and he braced himself for the struggle to come. He did not have long to wait; in January of 1951, Giap launched his forces, now organized in divisions, against the Red River Delta in a series of massive attacks which continued until June. It was one of Giap's few miscalculations: the French fought well and the Vietminh lost heavily, not only in the Tonkin where the Catholics sided with the French, but also in Cochinchina where a sacrificial diversionary offensive effectively eliminated the mostly non-communist Vietminh. Having stopped the Vietminh divisions, de Lattre went over to the offensive, launching his forces against the town of Hoa Binh south of the Red River Delta in mid-November. At first the French were successful; paratroops quickly seized the town and linked up with armored forces driving southwest from the delta down RC 6 and with a riverine force of gunboats and landing craft pressing down the Black River from the north. Hoa Binh was the

The Dien Bien Phu campaign soon became bogged down in siege operations for which the French were ill prepared. Note the thin barbed-wire entanglement.

capital of the Muong Tribe, who were friendly to the French, and the move seemed astute politically, but things quickly turned sour. Giap refused to give battle and the Vietminh melted away, only to reappear in carefully planned ambushes that took an increasingly heavy French toll as the months wore on. In January 1952, the French, with little to show for their losses, had to withdraw; by the end of February they were back inside the de Lattre Line. In the meantime, de Lattre himself was evacuated to France, terminally ill with cancer. He died weeks before the final French withdrawal.

The Hoa Binh offensive was the high point of French military fortunes. With the onset of the dry monsoon in October, the Vietminh emerged from their base areas in the Bac Viet and crossed the upper Red River to invade the Tai highlands. The Tai tribes had rallied to the French in 1947 and their allegiance was one of the few French political successes, but little had been done to capitalize on it and within weeks Giap's divisions had swept it away. A French counteroffensive against communist supply lines northwest of the Red River Delta in November penetrated 120 miles into Vietminh territory and captured significant amounts of supplies, including Soviet-supplied trucks, but it failed to distract Giap from his prize. As with Hoa Binh, the Vietminh refused to stand and fight; initially easy French gains were followed by increasingly severe ambushes and the French were back to their start line within a month. It had been an exercise in futility.

Meanwhile, and of more pressing concern to the French high command, the Vietminh pressed on into Laos, seizing Thakek on the Thai border and threatening the Royal capital of Luang Prabang. Luang Prabang did not fall, saved by the onset of the wet monsoon in late April, but it was a near thing and a major embarrassment for the French, for whom tranquil Laos had been one of the few bright spots in a gloomy picture.

Several weeks later, a new commander in chief, Lieutenant General Henri Navarre, arrived from Paris. Intelligent and energetic, though with a distant, even cold personality – an associate described him as "feline" in temperament – Navarre understood that time was running out for the French. Casualties among the regular forces had caused little outcry, but expenditures on the war continued to mount with little to show in return and French political patience was running thin. Navarre consulted with his theater commander in Tonkin, Major General René Cogny, and resolved to stake everything on a final roll of the dice, confident that if he raised the stakes high enough he could draw Giap's divisions into battle and crush them with superior firepower. He predicted victory in words that were to haunt his American successors: "Now we can see it clearly – like light at the end of a tunnel."

Navarre's plan was calculated to solve several

On 17 April, 1954, a spotlessly turned-out General Nguyen Van Hinh, Chief of Staff of the Vietnamese National Army, reviews his troops with Bao Dai. More French than Vietnamese, Hinh inspired little confidence.

Too little and too late: the Douglas B-26 was a good ground-attack aircraft, but the French received only a few, and then only during the spring of 1954.

In the aftermath of Dien Bien Phu, medics unload wounded from an American H-19 which has landed on the airstrip at Luang Prabang in Laos. The French received only a handful of U.S. helicopters.

Right: French and Vietnamese survivors of Dien Bien Phu, photographed by a Soviet cameraman, on their way to Vietminh prison camps; most died along the way.

Below: negotiators at work in Geneva, June 1954. Sitting at left are Britain's Anthony Eden and the Soviet delegate, V. Molotov; Chou En-lai is at the rear and the French Prime Minister, Pierre Mendès-France, at right.

As the withdrawal from the Red River Delta proceeds during July 1954, a soldier of the French Union Forces looks down on Phat Diem cathedral, already in communist hands.

problems at once. He would insert a major French force deep within Vietminh territory by air, blocking the invasion route to Laos, providing a base to support partisan operations behind communist lines and forcing Giap to give battle. The location which he and Cogny selected for their airhead was a former provincial seat in a river valley near the Laotian border, Dien Bien Phu. To command the operation, Navarre selected Colonel Christian de Castries a dashing, highly decorated cavalryman with a brilliant record, seemingly the ideal choice to lead the slashing raids into communist territory which Navarre and Cogny envisioned.

The operation began on 20 November, 1953, when three parachute battalions dropped into the Dien Bien Phu basin, which they seized against light opposition. The French quickly built an airstrip and began flying in troops and materiel, including six light tanks transported in pieces and assembled on the spot. Engineers

constructed a system of defensive strongholds, which Castries named for his mistresses. A stream of VIPs and experts, including senior U.S. military officers, inspected the position and pronounced it sound.

For a time all seemed well, but Navarre had badly underestimated the Vietminh. Within weeks, French forces attempting to move out of the valley met ambushes which became progressively more intense. By February they were confined to the basin. In the meantime the Vietminh had routed the Tai partisans, and the demoralized survivors who straggled in from the north were of little value. Then, on 13 March, the most basic flaw in Navarre's plan became evident when Vietminh artillery opened up from the surrounding hills, immediately closing the airfield. Dien Bien Phu was isolated except for resupply by airdrop. The French gunners were unable to locate the camouflaged communist guns and the artillery commander committed suicide. The outlying

Combat engineers blow up a causeway in July 1954. French forces in Tonkin continued to withdraw systematically as the diplomats approached agreement in Geneva.

Right: emaciated French soldiers line the rail of a landing craft after their release from Vietminh captivity in July 1954. Prisoners of the Vietminh received no medical treatment and most died.

The first Vietminh soldiers cross the Paul Doumer bridge (below) on 9 October, 1954, to take control of Hanoi in accordance with the Geneva agreement. French liaison officers stand in the background.

positions of Gabrielle, Beatrice and Anne-Marie were quickly overrun and Vietminh sappers began driving trenches toward the central position in a reversion to eighteenth century siege warfare. Supply shortages loomed as communist anti-aircraft guns – another surprise – forced the resupply drops to higher altitudes, littering the valley floor with parachutes and gratuitously supplying the Vietminh.

Having prepared poorly, the French fought well. Castries, psychologically unfit for grinding siege operations, suffered a breakdown, relinquishing de facto command to a cabal of junior paratroop officers. The morale of the Algerian and Moroccan units cracked at the end, but the paratroops, Foreign Legionnaires, tank crews and gunners fought on with skill and tenacity. There was never a shortage of volunteers to parachute into the doomed fortress, including hundreds of Vietnamese, and the one French surprise for the Vietminh was their ability to mount effective counterattacks. As late as 10 April, the French recaptured a key stronghold at the northeast corner of Elaine and there is evidence that the Vietminh suffered a serious crisis of morale.

November 1954: another transfer of power begins in South Vietnam, as U.S. Presidential Envoy General J. Lawton Collins (right, in the center) deplanes at Saigon's Tan Son Nhut Airport and is greeted by a grim-faced French High Commissioner, General Jouhaud (to the right).

As the French withdraw from Tonkin, a confident Ho Chi Minh (left) smiles for the press in the Vietminh capital of Thai Nguyen, in early October 1954.

While the issue was not as preordained as is generally supposed, French miscalculation had put the garrison in a position whereby only a miracle could save it ... and, indeed, a "miracle" was proposed in the form of saturation bombing of the Vietminh positions by U.S. air power, an idea seriously considered in President Eisenhower's inner circle. Additional American aid was offered and aircraft deliveries increased sharply in March and April. But it was too little and too late.

As April slipped away, the Vietminh grip on Dien Bien Phu tightened inexorably. During the night of 6-7 May, 1954, a huge mine pulverized the remains of stronghold Elaine and there was nothing left with which to meet the communist assault. Castries surrendered, and dawn saw Vietminh assault troops waving flags atop his command bunker. Some 7,000 prisoners were marched off to camps in the Bac Viet and northern Annam; nearly half of them were to die en route. France was finished in Vietnam. President Mendès-France entered into negotiations with the Vietminh in Geneva and on 21 July, 1954, at 0343, Geneva time, he signed the accord that marked the formal end of the French phase of the Vietnam War.

In a sense it was a curious accord. Ho did not get all he wanted, nor even all he could have reasonably expected. The French military position was weaker than even the numbers implied, for the losses at Dien Bien Phu included the *crème de la crème* of the French forces. Vietminh infiltration of the Red River Delta had reached alarming proportions and, as Dien Bien Phu surrendered, the main French mobile force in the Central Highlands was being cut to pieces near Pleiku. Yielding to pressure from Soviet Foreign Minister Molotov and his Chinese counterpart Chou En-lai, conscious of Soviet and Chinese strategic vulnerabilities and anxious to placate the western democracies, Ho had to be content with the northern half of his country. It was an unstable situation which could not endure.

CHAPTER THREE
THE ADVISORY PHASE

American involvement in Indochina built up slowly and incrementally, and was at first all but invisible to most citizens. In World War II, Vietnam was a backwater so far as the U.S. military was concerned; little went on there which was of any great consequence to the overall effort against Japan, and American officials charged with prosecuting the war in Southeast Asia characteristically gave little thought as to how their efforts might determine the shape of the postwar world. Perhaps ironically, the United States became involved in Vietnam even before the outbreak of armed hostilities between the French and Vietminh. In the final months of World War II, the Office of Strategic Services (OSS), precursor to the CIA, had parachuted a small team into Vietnam to make contact with local elements resisting the Japanese with the intention of providing assistance to shot-down American aviators. The team, under Major Archimedes Patty, had made contact with the Vietminh and Patty himself was at Ho Chi Minh's side when the latter proclaimed Vietnamese independence on 2 September, 1945. In later years, some analysts were to maintain that Patti, in conveying the impression of U.S. endorsement of Ho Chi Minh, played a crucial role in swinging popular support behind the Vietminh.

In the wake of V-J Day, American awareness of Southeast Asia and Vietnam diminished from little to next to nothing, yet even as America withdrew seemingly inexorable forces were at work which were to draw the United States into the Vietnamese quagmire. American hopes for a benign postwar international order based on the United Nations were dashed by intransigent Soviet imperialism in eastern Europe and by the triumph of Mao Tse Tung's Communists over Chiang Kai-shek's American-supported nationalists in China. Winston Churchill's Iron Curtain speech in March of 1946 marked the beginning of the Cold War and President Harry Truman's momentous decision in 1948 to provide aid and sustenance to the Greek government in its struggle against communist guerrillas was a watershed in international relations, marking the practical beginning of the policy of containment of communism. As American policy shifted from one of hopeful optimism to containment, the French struggle in Indochina changed in character from a campaign of colonial reconquest to a crusade against communism. It was against this backdrop that the Soviet-supplied North Korean Peoples Army invaded South Korea on 25 June, 1950, a move that was followed immediately by President Truman's decision to commit U.S. ground forces to resist them. With American forces actively in combat against a communist enemy in Asia, official attitudes toward the French in Indochina completed the shift from unabashed hostility to the re-imposition of colonial rule – an attitude of which President Franklin Roosevelt was a major exponent – to increased willingness to aid allies in a common struggle. By the time the Truman Administration gave way to that of Republican Dwight Eisenhower in 1953, the shift was complete. Eisenhower entered office with a mandate to secure an end to hostilities in Korea on which he soon made good, but the basic foundations of American foreign policy remained essentially the same.

Between 1950 and the French collapse at Dien Bien Phu, U.S. aid swelled from a trickle to a torrent. The increased flow of money and materiel was accompanied by a parallel traffic in high-level dignitaries who toured the French positions, including Dien Bien Phu itself. But even assuming that the French could have cobbled together a viable political strategy capable of containing the Vietminh appeal to anti-colonialist nationalism, it was too little and too late. Significantly, the bulk of American aircraft deliveries to the French took place after March of 1954 and, symbolically, two French Foreign Legion battalions that had fought in Korea under U.S./United Nations command were destroyed in June of 1954 as part of the principal French mobile reaction force in the Central Highlands of South Vietnam. As awareness of the gravity of the situation sank in at the

With all the optimism of youth, smiling children wait for the Vietminh victory parade in Hanoi, on 14 November, 1954. They hold a communist flag above their heads for shade.

Some 860,000 refugees, 600,000 of them Catholics and most of the rest comprising government officials, soldiers and their families, fled the North. Though the majority of refugees departed by ship, others were flown south in French and U.S. aircraft.

highest levels, desperate measures were proposed, including a massive application of air power against the Vietminh at Dien Bien Phu; even the atomic bomb was mentioned in this regard, though there is no convincing evidence that the nuclear option was seriously considered within the upper echelons of the Eisenhower Administration. Ultimately, domestic political considerations and a lack of confidence in French policies and competence turned President Eisenhower from overt U.S. military involvement. Ironically, Senator Lyndon B. Johnson of Texas was apparently instrumental in persuading Eisenhower not to intervene. The only American casualties in the French phase of the war were a handful of civilian airmen flying under contract to the French, who were shot down over Dien Bien Phu in

Refugees disembark in Saigon in mid-April 1955. The last refugee-laden French ship cleared Haiphong harbor on 15 May, 1955.

desperate eleventh-hour attempts to drop supplies to the doomed garrison.

Still, awareness of the American stake in Vietnam was growing. On 7 April, 1954, a month to the day before the fall of Dien Bien Phu, President Dwight D. Eisenhower, speaking at a press conference, drew on an earlier utterance by his predecessor Harry Truman in comparing the nations of Southeast Asia to a row of dominos, suggesting that communist victory in Vietnam would result in the fall of Laos, Thailand and Burma and threaten the rest of the region. Eisenhower's utterance was a warning of things to come, but in the event diplomatic and political realities were to defuse for a time the underlying realities behind the domino analogy, for the French did far better diplomatically at Geneva than they had militarily in Indochina. President Pierre Mendès-France negotiated a cease-fire that limited Ho Chi Minh and the Vietminh to control of Vietnam north of the 17th Parallel, preserving Laos, Cambodia and South Vietnam as independent republics. In this, he was aided by Soviet Foreign Minister Vyacheslav Molotov and his Chinese colleague Chou En-lai who, dealing from positions of perceived weakness and eager to allay Western fears about communist expansion, pressured Ho and his delegation to accept much less than they might reasonably have expected. In addition, the agreement included a population exchange provision which permitted free travel between the communist north and the south for a limited period of time.

The Geneva Accords incorporated a series of carefully phased withdrawals and disengagements to be monitored by an International Control Commission (ICC) formed from Polish, Indian and Canadian military contingents. Even before the document was signed, French forces in North Vietnam had begun pulling back to their final positions around Hanoi and Haiphong. The victorious Vietminh did not enter Hanoi until 9 October and the French held the port of Haiphong until May of 1955. In the interim, U.S. agents of the new Central Intelligence Agency (CIA) went to work behind French lines, spreading propaganda and sabotaging equipment shortly to fall into the hands of the victorious Vietminh. Perhaps their most noteworthy success was persuading Catholics to flee to the south; of the 860,000 or so people who fled the north, as many as 600,000 were Catholics. In the south, Vietminh cadres went underground or moved north as religious sects, nationalists and Bao Dai adherents scrambled for power, fighting across a political landscape that bore the imprint of seven decades of divisive French policies. The onset of total chaos was arrested by the appearance on the scene of one of the strangest political leaders ever to walk the stage of history, Ngo Dinh Diem.

The son of a councillor to Bao Dai's father, Emperor Than Thai, Diem received a French education and served briefly in the French colonial government during the early 1930s before resigning in protest over the French refusal to grant meaningful power to Vietnamese officials. A political activist and an ardent nationalist, Diem had refused an offer to serve in the Japanese puppet government in 1945. A devout Catholic and a staunch anti-communist, he subsequently rejected a similar offer by Ho Chi Minh. But Diem's family was large, powerful and well-connected – his elder brother Ngo Dinh Thuc had entered the priesthood and risen to the position of Bishop of Vinh Long in South Vietnam – so Diem was not without supporters or resources. In 1950, and still a relative unknown, he traveled to the United States, where he met numbers of influential Americans including Francis Cardinal Spellman and senators John F. Kennedy and Mike Mansfield. When, during the 1954 Geneva negotiations, he accepted Emperor Bao Dai's offer to become Prime Minister of what was to be the Republic of Vietnam, he quickly demonstrated surprising willpower along with a good measure of luck – aided by American support at several critical junctures – in consolidating his power.

In a series of astonishing political twists and turns, between the Geneva Accords and the fall of 1955, Diem

Paratroops engage Binh Xuyen gunmen in Saigon, in late April 1955. To the astonishment of most observers, Ngo Dinh Diem's challenge to the Binh Xuyen succeeded.

became the unchallenged political leader of South Vietnam. With the assistance of well-timed Saigon street demonstrations orchestrated by his younger brother Ngo Dinh Nhu, he convinced the Americans that he was a credible national leader, insuring the indispensable sanction and support of the United States. Diem's first serious challenge came from the French-backed Binh Xuyen, who controlled Saigon's gambling and vice syndicates and maintained a sizeable private army. Bolstered by American Air Force Colonel Edward Lansdale, he ordered the nascent South Vietnamese Army against the Binh Xuyen in April of 1955. To the astonishment of informed onlookers, the ARVN (Army of the Republic of Viet Nam) defeated the Binh Xuyen in a series of battles that left 500 dead and thousands homeless. By May, Binh Xuyen leader Bay Vien was in exile in Paris and the remnants of his forces had fled to the Mekong Delta where they joined the Vietminh. Even before his destruction of the Binh Xuyen, Diem had begun to move against the religious sects, the Hoa Hao

Ho Chi Minh arrives in Moscow (below) to be greeted by Soviet President Voroshilov (to the left). As Diem consolidated his power in the South, Ho Chi Minh traveled abroad to shore up his alliances.

Above: the wife of Hoa Hao leader Tran Van Soai reviews female militia in the summer of 1955.

我吃東西細細

嘴臉楷袖

的嚼碎了統吶

下去

A Nationalist Chinese sponsored school in May 1956. In the prevailing political turmoil, efforts to promote development in newly-independent South Vietnam lacked focus.

them came to appreciate the political complexities of the situation in which they found themselves. What they did not do was to communicate that appreciation successfully to their military and political superiors.

Meanwhile, the north was undergoing a series of upheavals under its new leaders. The ravages of war had left the north severely short of food, and only huge shipments of Burmese rice paid for with Soviet credits prevented mass starvation in 1955. As soon as Ho's cadres took power in Hanoi, an internal struggle broke out between a "southern" faction, which wanted to pursue the armed struggle to unify the country by initiating military operations in the south at the earliest moment, and a "northern" faction, including Giap, which argued for putting the north on a proper economic and political footing first. In the event the southern faction won, but the debate took time and in the meantime North Vietnam was swept up in the throes of a land reform and collectivization campaign which wreaked havoc on the fragile social peace that had accompanied the euphoria of victory over the hated French. To identify "class enemies," the Communist Party passed decrees which divided the populace on the basis of elaborate classification schemes based on detailed comparisons of numbers of hectares tilled, quarts of rice held, salaries earned and paid and numbers of piglets owned. The irony was that of all Vietnam the north, where some ninety-eight percent of the peasantry owned the land which they tilled, was least in need of land reform.

In the event, widespread resentment of high-handed cadres and fear of the arbitrariness of the classification decrees and the tribunals that enforced them broke out into mass disturbances in several areas. The worst of these erupted in early November 1956 in the form of open resistance among the peasantry Ho Chi Minh's home province of Nghe An, witnessed by Canadian ICC members. So threatening was the situation that the North Vietnamese government, like the French colonial regime faced by a similar situation a quarter of a century earlier, ordered in the Army. The 325th Division restored order at a cost of many thousands of peasants killed and imprisoned, lower estimates running to about 6,000 victims. The carnage was considerable, but went all but ignored in a world preoccupied simultaneously with the Suez Crisis and the Hungarian uprising. President Ho Chi Minh publicly apologized for the excesses and the program was toned down; all of this took time, but failed to stay the inexorable logic of war. By the spring of 1957, the "southern" faction had won out: in March, the 12th Vietnamese Communist Party Plenum ordered universal military conscription, and the beginning of hostilities in the south was not far behind. By August, guerrillas were mounting attacks on isolated government-controlled villages and outposts and and by October, the Viet Cong could field substantial guerrilla forces.

and Cao Dai. With a combination of military force and police state coercion, orchestrated by his younger brother Ngo Dinh Nhu, he succeeded in neutralizing them politically and incorporating their militias into the ARVN. Finally, in a blatantly rigged national election, Diem forced the electorate to chose between him and the discredited Bao Dai.

Ngo Dinh Diem's assumption of the Presidency on 26 October, 1955, marked the birth of the Republic of South Vietnam, and even his detractors had to admit that he had demonstrated amazing staying power. The execution of imprisoned Hoa Hao leader Ba Cut and the departure of the last French troops the following April seemingly put the seal of permanence on his regime. Following his victory over the sects, Diem moved against Vietminh remnants and revolutionary opponents with his *To Cong* ("Denounce the Communists") campaign which, in prevailing turmoil, achieved some considerable success in rooting out Vietminh cadres. Diem also achieved a rare victory over the communists in the war of ideas by successfully labeling the southern communists Viet Cong, a derogatory appellation meaning Vietnamese Communist. He petitioned President Eisenhower for military assistance and advisors; advisors came, teaching their Vietnamese charges the complexities of weapons systems, and the skills required to operate them, along with organizational schemes and tactics. Some few of

The difficulties in the north produced a breathing space, but Diem and his government, after a promising start, proved unable to exploit the advantage. The difficulties began with Diem himself. A closed, private personality he had little sense of priorities and an almost paranoid fear of being overthrown. He tended to trust only Catholics and placed enormous power and trust in the hands of his family, producing serious internal stresses in the Army and government. Though Diem himself was driven by patriotism and was personally incorruptible, the same could not be said for all of his relatives, and corruption and blatant favoritism flourished as his family and Catholics appointees – most of them northern refugees – assumed the lion's share of power. His secretive and manipulative younger brother Nhu became his right-hand man and, in the view of some, his evil genius; his elder brother Thuc rose to become Archbishop of Hue and head of the Church in the South, and his younger brother Ngo Dinh Can, though he held no official position, carved out for himself what amounted to a fiefdom as de facto governor of Hue. The government and army became polarized along religious lines as "dependable" Catholics received the plum posts regardless of ability or demonstrated competence. Particularly obnoxious to many was Ngo's wife, Madame Ngo Dinh Nhu, who, since Diem never married, became to all intents and purposes the first lady of South Vietnam. Beautiful, possessed of an acid tongue, insensitive, and utterly intolerant of those whose beliefs diverged from her own, she became a potent symbol of the degree to which the Diem regime was out of touch with those whom it governed. Her characterization of the self-immolation of Buddhist monks protesting Diem's religious policies in the summer of 1963 as "Buddhist barbecues" gave the regime a well-deserved notoriety in the world press.

Preoccupied with the threat of a coup, neither Diem nor his brother Nhu seems to have recognized the growing seriousness of the insurgent threat, whose roots lay as much in the inequities of their regime as in the machinations of the communist leadership in the north. True, they attempted to profit from the lessons of the successful British counterinsurgency in Malaya by concentrating the peasantry in relatively large, well-defended villages. The first experiment with this concept, the so-called Agrovilles, was initiated in 1959 and withered away in the face of massive hostility among those whom it was supposed to benefit. The experience served mainly to demonstrate just how little understanding the Diem regime had of the aspirations and fears of the peasantry. A similar display of lack of realism was demonstrated in the regime's official ideology, Nhu's "Personalist" movement, a weird combination of French philosophical ideas, communist organization and fascist tactics, which served over the short term as a useful prop to the regime but utterly failed to attract any following beyond the mandatory membership that was a concomitant of government employment.

By 1959, the weaknesses of the Diem regime had combined with growing Viet Cong confidence and competence to produce the makings of an incipient crisis, though few American observers discerned its dimensions. Diem had followed the expulsion of French forces with a request for American aid and military advisors and by the end of 1959 there were just over 750 U.S. military personnel in South Vietnam. At the same time, the number of terrorist incidents and assassinations of government officials had grown exponentially and, on 8 July, 1959, a Viet Cong attack on Bien Hoa air base killed a U.S. Army major and a master sergeant, the first American combat casualties in Vietnam since the immediate aftermath of World War II. At this pivotal juncture the United States, upon whom Diem and South Vietnam depended, underwent a change of leadership: on 8 November, 1960, Democratic Senator John F. Kennedy defeated Vice President Richard M. Nixon in the presidential election, to replace Dwight Eisenhower as President. By the time the new President was inaugurated on 20 January, 1960, the communists had announced the establishment of the National Liberation Front, the political arm of the Viet Cong, which was set up to provide organization and leadership to dissidents of whatever stripe who were prepared to fight for the overthrow of the Diem regime. Few recognized it at the time, but America was at war.

Ho Chi Minh and Soviet leader Nikita Khruschev meet in Moscow on 3 July, 1959. Though fiercely independent in their policies, Ho and his colleagues took care to be on good terms with their revolutionary brothers in Moscow and Peking.

CHAPTER FOUR
PRESIDENT KENNEDY'S WAR

General Paul B. Harkins (second from right), Chief of the newly-established U.S. Military Assistance Command, is greeted on his arrival in Saigon on 18 February, 1962, by Major General Charles Timmed (left) and South Vietnamese Army Chief of Staff, General Le Van Ty. Behind Le Van Ty is Frederick E. Nolting, U.S. ambassador to Vietnam.

A harbinger of things to come: an Army lieutenant swears in new recruits (left) at a New York City draft induction center on 27 July, 1961.

John Fitzgerald Kennedy's victory in the November 1960 presidential election was welcomed by many who saw the dynamic young President as a refreshing departure from the legacies of the Cold War, John Foster Dulles' brinksmanship and the intellectual stagnation of the Eisenhower years. Under the rubric of The New Frontier, the incoming Democratic administration promised to seek new and innovative solutions to the problems of America and the world. Kennedy's election was widely viewed as cause for hope, not only in the United States but throughout the world. Among his earliest acts as President were a number of senior appointments by which he signalled his determination to implement policies which, if not as sharply divergent from those of the past as many perceived, he intended to pursue with unprecedented determination and vigor. At his inauguration on January 21, 1961, he named Dean Rusk Secretary of State, Robert Strange McNamara Secretary of Defense and McGeorge Bundy National Security Policy Adviser. A salient characteristic of war is the manner in which it gives play to personalities at the top, taxing strengths, magnifying foibles and seeking out weaknesses with a seemingly human intelligence, and all of these men

were to leave the imprint of their personalities on the Vietnam War.

Among the first and most serious foreign policy challenges to confront the new President and his team of subordinates and advisors were those of Southeast Asia. Particularly threatening was the situation in Laos where Pathet Lao insurgents threatened to overturn the 1954 Geneva Accords. In August, with the American Presidential campaign in full swing, a neutralist paratroop coup had overthrown the rightist Vientiane regime. Chaos ensued as the Soviets intervened with aid for the insurgents. Kennedy responded by sending military aid and U.S. Army Special Forces advisors, while at the same time pursuing behind-the-scenes diplomatic initiatives. The situation did not at once improve, and in the spring of 1962 Kennedy dispatched troops and air power to northern Thailand to reassure the Thais, to serve as an implied threat and as a safeguard against communist victory. Eventually Kennedy's combination of firmness and restraint paid off: the military situation stabilized, and Britain and the Soviet Union reconvened the Geneva Conference to negotiate an end to the crisis. On 23 July, 1962, the parties to the Geneva Conference signed a series of accords under which Laos was to be ruled by a neutralist government under Prince Souvanna Phouma – whom the Eisenhower administration had considered too accommodating to the communists – with rightist and Pathet Lao participation. The Geneva Formula proved amazingly enduring; Souvanna Phouma was to serve as Premier of a nominally neutral, but in fact increasingly anti-communist, government for another twelve years. At the same time, the Formula papered over an unpleasant military reality. Most of eastern Laos was under North Vietnamese control, notably the vital lines of communication and resupply linking North Vietnam with Viet Cong staging areas in the Central Highlands of South Vietnam and along the Cambodian border, the Ho Chi Minh Trail.

But as the Kennedy Administration struggled toward a resolution of the Laotian crisis, the situation in Vietnam continued to deteriorate. Even before the new President's

inauguration, Diem came within an ace of being overthrown by paratroops led by junior officers concerned with his regime's corruption and their ineffectiveness in dealing with the Viet Cong. The coup was put down with difficulty and a dash of luck, and the problems that had prompted it continued to fester. Increasingly preoccupied with the fear of being overthrown, Diem and his brother Ngo Dinh Nhu concentrated power in the hands of those personally obligated to them. In practical terms, this meant that positions of authority in the government and army were filled with the scions of well-to-do families who had assimilated French culture, and northerners, Catholics and Diem family loyalists were disproportionately over-represented. The political distance between the regime and those it governed widened, and the effectiveness of the nascent ARVN (Army of the Republic of Vietnam) atrophied.

Right: Vietnamese student pilots with their U.S. Air Force instructor at Moody AFB, Georgia, in July 1964. Increasing numbers of Vietnamese officers and NCOs were sent to the U.S. for training.

Right: Marines sent to Thailand in response to the Laotian crisis, in April 1962. Vietnam was only one of many problems confronting President Kennedy when he took office.

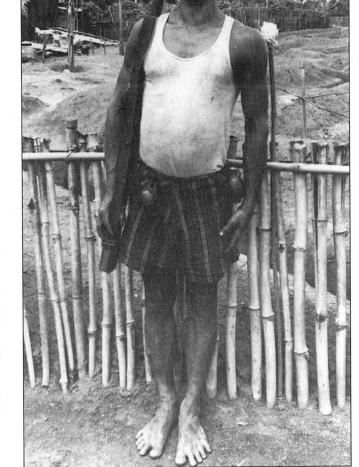

Below: a montagnard militiaman at a Special Forces camp, in September 1962. Like the French, the U.S. enjoyed some success in mobilizing tribal minorities against the Vietnamese communists.

But Diem was far more effective in dealing with Americans than with his compatriots, and the weaknesses of his regime were not immediately apparent to U.S. observers. For a time, therefore, American efforts to shore up the Vietnamese bulwark against communist expansion continued along time-honored lines. In the political sphere, these focused on nation building, the work of advisors and technical experts in government administration, police work, agriculture and banking. In the military sphere, they focused on the provision of logistics and weaponry, supported by technical training missions and advisors. U.S. Army advisors oversaw the creation of a South Vietnamese military with an organizational structure which duplicated the American model. The country was divided into military districts under corps headquarters, each containing two or more divisions. Along with U.S. tables of organization, the ARVN received American weapons and training which, critics would argue, was better suited to mechanized operations on the plains of Europe than to a guerrilla struggle in the jungles and swamps of Vietnam.

The crisis in Southeast Asia was not the only problem which the Democratic Administration had inherited from its predecessor. Cuba had fallen under the sway of Fidel Castro in 1959 and Castro had turned out to be not a middle class reformer but a communist revolutionary.

South Vietnamese troops board U.S. Army H-21s, in early 1963. Using "advisors" to provide helicopter mobility was a quick and politically palatable way to increase ARVN effectiveness.

Included in the Eisenhower Administration's legacy to its successor was a plan for Castro's military overthrow through an invasion by a CIA-trained emigré force based in Anastasio Somoza's Nicaragua. Kennedy went ahead with the plan in April of 1961, only to see it become a fiasco. Embarrassment over the transparent falseness of the official cover story that the initial air strikes were mounted by defectors from Castro's Air Force caused Kennedy to cancel subsequent strikes. As a result, a handful of Cuban fighter planes survived to put the invasion convoy to flight, leading to the isolation and surrender of the force put ashore at the Bay of Pigs. From the standpoint of Vietnam, the failure had two significant consequences. First, in the inevitable finger-pointing which followed, Kennedy loyalists attempted to shift blame to the military by pointing out that the JCS (Joint Chiefs of Staff) had endorsed the invasion plan, which they had … on condition that air superiority was maintained, a condition negated by Kennedy's decision to abort the follow-up air attacks. In retrospect, this was the first, small fracture in the bond of trust between the military and the civilian leadership of the executive branch. Personalities played a major role in the matter, for Secretary of Defense McNamara and the youthful civilian assistants whom he brought into the upper echelons of the Department of Defense – the so-called Whiz Kids – made no secret of their scorn for the professional military and what they regarded as its

An armed T-28 trainer on patrol. Fixed-wing air power provided by Air Force Air Commandos was an important part of the Kennedy buildup.

ARVN rangers board a Marine H-34 in the Central Highlands. Marine H-34s were sent to Soc Trang in the Mekong Delta in April 1962. The H-34 was the best reciprocating-engined helicopter of the war.

A cadre rehearses an attack on a sand table model of a government outpost. The Viet Cong pitted discipline and painstakingly detailed planning against U.S. technology.

sloppy, unstructured decision-making. Second, and more important over the short term, the Bay of Pigs left Kennedy with little maneuvering room in Southeast Asia. The Republicans had made much political capital portraying the Democrats as the party that "lost China" to communism, and any decision to abandon South Vietnam would inevitably carry a high political price for any Democratic President.

Then, in the autumn of 1962, as the consequences of the Bay of Pigs sank in, a bellicose Soviet Union under Premier Nikita Khruschev decided to test the new American President by installing nuclear-tipped intermediate range ballistic missiles in Cuba, apparently to provide leverage to force political concessions in Europe. The resultant Cuban Missile Crisis is generally considered the Kennedy Administration's finest hour. Working in close harmony with his inner circle of confidants and advisors, Kennedy orchestrated a political offensive in the United Nations and the world press, and a naval blockade of Cuba and threatened military action against the island to force the Soviets to back down and withdraw their missiles. Cynics might argue that Kennedy extracted little from the Soviets in the ensuing settlement, but he had avoided nuclear war without sacrificing essential American interests. His Administration's image, tarnished at the Bay of Pigs, regained much of its luster. Of importance for the future, Kennedy's inner circle of advisors, notably Secretary of Defense McNamara, became confident of their ability to manage crises in a rational, measured manner. Their confidence was to be put to the test in Vietnam.

While America was in political transition, North Vietnam's leaders had not remained inert. Carefully monitoring events in the south, they orchestrated a careful buildup of guerrilla cadres, to be backed at the appropriate time by the commitment of regular Viet Cong and North Vietnamese forces. In May of 1959, the 15th Plenum of the Vietnamese Communist Party concluded that the moment was at hand to initiate armed struggle in the south, and line-of-communications troops were sent into southern Laos to open the Ho Chi Minh Trail. Within months, Vietminh cadres who had fled north in 1955 began working their way south along the network of paths and waterways to reassemble the

Right: forcibly relocated villagers, August 1962. In response to the guerrilla menace, the Diem regime moved to concentrate the rural populace in so-called strategic hamlets.

Left: a PAVN instructor and recruits armed with U.S. M-1 carbines in Quang Nam Province near Da Nang. Until 1965, communist guerrillas in the south were armed with a diverse assortment of captured weapons.

Below: the aftermath of Ap Bac. Two shattered UH-1B helicopters lie in a rice paddy. Viet Cong gunners at Ap Bac downed four helicopters in five minutes.

Officers and men (above) of the 57th Transport Company (Light Helicopter) pay their final respects to a crew chief killed in action in October 1962 – one of the first of many.

insurgent apparatus. The number of assassinations and kidnappings of government officials and other terrorist incidents in South Vietnam rose exponentially during 1959. By the spring of 1960, Viet Cong forces were operating in battalion strength in the Mekong Delta, and North Vietnam had initiated conscription. These military moves were, in a sense, a prelude to the overt declaration of political intent which was made on 20 December, 1960, with the announcement of the formation of the National Liberation Front, a communist-sponsored political umbrella organization for those who, for whatever reason, desired the overthrow of the Diem regime and a shadow government for the south.

The new administration in Washington recognized the insurgent character of the conflict, nor was it blind to the liabilities of the Diem government. On 28 January, 1961, as the upsurge of revolutionary activity continued, President Kennedy approved a counterinsurgency plan for Vietnam which called for government reform and a restructured military as the basis for expanded U.S. assistance. In May, the President approved an increase in the size of the Military Assistance Advisory Group based in Saigon and ordered the dispatch of some 400 Army Special Forces troopers to Vietnam, where they were to operate under Central Intelligence Agency control. In a series of intricate maneuvers, Kennedy and McNamara explored available military options with the JCS (Joint Chiefs of Staff), securing from the latter in May of 1961 the recommendation that American troops should be sent to Vietnam if the administration intended to draw the line of containment in Southeast Asia. The

Helicopter mobility hurt the Viet Cong badly, but they took its measure in the battle of Ap Bac, on 3 January, 1963. Right: Army personnel unload a wounded Vietnamese soldier after the battle.

qualifier was, of course, a political condition, throwing the ball back into the President's court. Having exhausted traditional channels, Kennedy now moved with dispatch, appointing General Maxwell Taylor as Military Representative to the President and sending him to South Vietnam with Deputy National Security Adviser Walt Rostow in October 1961. As Chief of Staff of the Army during the Eisenhower Administration, Taylor had fought unsuccessfully to preserve the Army's traditional pre-eminence in the defense establishment. After retiring in 1959, he had written an influential book, *The Uncertain Trumpet*, which criticized what he considered to be America's over-reliance on nuclear deterrence and called for a strategy of flexible response. Taylor's message found a receptive reader in John Kennedy, and he was to find himself at the center of policy formulation with regard to Vietnam.

In Saigon, Taylor and Rostow were quickly apprised of the deteriorating military situation. Taylor sent a series of cables to the President alerting him to the gravity of the situation. On 3 November, 1961, Taylor cabled a recommendation that three helicopter squadrons – roughly seventy-five helicopters – be sent to Vietnam to provide badly needed mobility to ARVN ground forces; he privately recommended that some 8,000 U.S. ground combat forces be sent as well. Taylor's cables sparked the beginning of the buildup of U.S. combat forces in Vietnam, but at the same time the President was receiving proposals from Under Secretary of State Chester Bowles and Averell Harriman, Chief American Negotiator at Geneva that a negotiated solution might be worked out along the lines of the Geneva Formula for Laos. Kennedy split the difference, opting to increase the U.S. military presence in Vietnam, though not by as much as Taylor had recommended and in ways calculated to preserve a relatively low political profile.

By late November, the first Air Force C-123 transport aircraft specially equipped to spray defoliants had departed the U.S. for South Vietnam. Potent AD-6 Skyraider fighter-bombers were given to the VNAF (Vietnamese Air Force). Amphibious M-113 APCs (armored personnel carriers) were provided to the ARVN, and were to prove useful in the waterlogged terrain of coastal Vietnam and the Mekong Delta. The Air Force sent a small number of hand-picked Air Commandos to Vietnam to train the fledgling VNAF and, under cover of their training role, to provide air support for government

Among the casualties of Ap Bac was the confidence of the U.S. press corps. UPI's Neil Sheehan (left) became increasingly skeptical of U.S. policy in the wake of Ap Bac.

Right: ARVN gunners with a new U.S. 155 mm howitzer. Heavy firepower was essential, but was no substitute for good training and high morale.

Paratroopers spill from U.S. Air Force C-123s near Tay Ninh, in March 1963. ARVN paratroopers were excellent soldiers, but their efforts were wasted because of the duplicity and inefficiency of Diem-appointed senior commanders.

Above: Buddhist leaders protest against government policies. Ngo Dinh Diem's final, fatal error lay in welding the Buddhists into a potent political force by his religious intolerance.

Left: ARVN officers display a captured Chinese-manufactured Moisin-Nagant rifle. Much ARVN effort in the Diem years went into carefully-orchestrated shows for U.S. advisors.

A pro-Diem demonstration mounted for the American media, in September 1963. Although brilliant political manipulators, Ngo Dinh Diem and his brother Ngo Dinh Ngu only commanded the allegiance of Catholics, civil servants and westernized elites.

Monks display signs protesting against the government's religious policies, in a demonstration on 18 August, 1963. The anger of the increasingly alienated Buddhists stood out against Diem's manipulations.

forces. The first armed T-28 piston-engined trainers arrived in November, shortly followed by twin-engined B-26 bombers. On 11 December, the escort carrier USS *Card* docked at Saigon transporting two U.S. Army helicopter companies equipped with a total of thirty-three CH-21 troop-transport helicopters between them. They were to be followed in April by a third squadron, this one provided by the Marines. Early in 1962, the Army introduced turbine-engined UH-1 "Huey" helicopters modified to carry machine guns and rockets, the first helicopter in Vietnam. On 23 December, 1961, U.S.

Army crewmen hook up an H-37 to an H-21 in September 1963. Many downed U.S. helicopters were recovered and returned to service. Characteristic of the freewheeling advisory years, the man at left is armed with a German WWII "burp gun."

The helicopter recovery continues as, with the lifting harness attached, a ground crewman gives the H-37 pilots the "clear to lift" signal.

Army helicopters carried ARVN troopers in a raid on a suspected Viet Cong radio transmitter west of Saigon. Though not billed as such at the time – officially American military personnel were advisors, not combatants – it was the first U.S. helicopter combat assault operation. Early in 1962, the U.S. Army introduced turbine-engined UH-1 "Huey" helicopters specially modified to carry machine guns and rockets, which were the first purpose-built helicopter gunships to see operational service. In April, a Marine helicopter squadron equipped with UH-34s joined the Army helicopter units.

U.S. advisors encouraged their Vietnamese counterparts to pursue the war against the elusive Viet Cong aggressively, and for a time air power and helicopter mobility gave the government forces a significant edge. Captured documents later indicated that the Viet Cong were hard pressed during 1962, and that same year the government initiated an ambitious Strategic Hamlet Program. Based on successful British experience in combating a communist-supported insurgency in Malaya, the Strategic Hamlets were intended to remove the peasantry from guerrilla-infested areas and concentrate them in large, well defended villages. Time was to reveal fatal shortcomings in the program, but for the moment it offered real promise.

When the MAAG Group was upgraded to Military Assistance Command Vietnam (MACV) under General Paul D. Harkins in February of 1962, seemingly favorable portents obscured serious underlying problems. The most basic of these was the communist determination to pursue the war to a victorious outcome, a determination which Americans invariably underestimated. The Viet Cong might be hurt by new American weapons and tactics, but they would learn and come back, backed, if need be, by cadres and regular units from the north. Of more immediate concern were the endemic weaknesses of the Diem regime which were just becoming apparent to the more perceptive American military advisors and reporters. These manifested themselves in a reluctance on the part of ARVN units to engage the communist foe aggressively, a product of Diem's practice of appointing commanders for political reliability rather than military competence and of deploying units as coup insurance rather than according to the dictates of the counterinsurgent war.

General Harkins and MACV maintained the position that the war was going well, and official deputations were taken to showpiece hamlets and treated to displays of ARVN determination and efficiency that had little to do with operational reality. Fissures began to appear in relations between the military in the field and the Pentagon. Distrustful of overly optimistic reports of progress in pacification, Secretary of Defense McNamara introduced an unequivocal standard: body count.

The H-37 heads for home with the rescued H-21 dangling below. The power of the reciprocating-engined H-37 is barely adequate for the rescue, so the H-21 has been stripped of every readily removable part.

A young Buddhist monk commits ritual suicide at a Saigon intersection. The self-immolation of Buddhist monks in protest against government policies, marked the beginning of the end for Ngo Dinh Diem.

Henceforth, operational and strategic success would be measured by the tally of enemy dead, and when it became evident that body counts were being inflated by the inclusion of civilian casualties, a count of captured weapons was required as well. But rather than introduce analytical rigor into the strategic calculus as McNamara had hoped, body count became a powerful corrupting influence. ARVN commanders quickly learned that high body counts were needed to make the Americans happy and U.S. advisors learned that they were necessary for promotion. Blatant abuses such as holding back weapons found in VC caches so that they could later be paired with civilian dead were not unknown; worse, body count became an end in itself, overriding the sophisticated political and operational calculations on which any successful counterinsurgency campaign must be based. In addition, Diem's near paranoid fear of a coup caused him to husband the strength of loyal units jealously; these were withheld from operations as coup insurance, and commanders quickly learned that the surest way to incur Diem's wrath was to sustain casualties. The result was operational stasis.

By mid-1962, perceptive U.S. advisors in the field were aware of deliberate ARVN foot-dragging and of its roots in Diem's political machinations, but they were unsuccessful in focusing MACV attention on the problem. The issues came dramatically to a head on 2 January, 1963, in the Battle of Ap Bac. Starting with an attack in seemingly overwhelming strength by the 7th ARVN Division on Viet Cong forces in the small hamlet of Bac on the eastern edge of the Plain of Reeds, the operation was orchestrated by the Senior U.S. Army Advisor to the 7th ARVN Division, Lt. Col. John Paul Vann. Planned to take advantage of helicopter mobility and the combat power of the APCs, it achieved surprise, catching a larger than expected communist force in its net. More importantly, the Viet Cong, hurt by the success of new government weapons and tactics, had decided to stand and fight to retain their credibility; for once the elusive guerrillas were in a position where they could be destroyed. But what should have been a major government victory turned into a fiasco through Diem's commanders' ineptitude, obstructionism and double-dealing. At the climax of the battle, Viet Cong machine gunners drove off the hitherto invincible M-113 APCs with hand grenades, in a desperate counterattack. Even then, an ARVN victory was in prospect, for the Viet Cong were surrounded on three sides and unable to retreat in daylight across open rice paddies in the face of air attack. But that prospect was dashed by the ARVN Division commander who, over Vann's livid protests, ordered the paratroop battalion held in reserve for just such a contingency to be dropped on the wrong side of the village, leaving the Viet Cong an open escape route. Vann decided to take his case discreetly but directly to

Repelled by the ghastly self-immolations of the monks and by Madame Nhu's reference to these suicides as "Buddhist barbecues," the Kennedy administration withdrew its support for Diem, after which his fall was not long in coming. Left: Presidential Palace guards under detention after the coup on 2 November, 1963.

Hero of the moment, General Tran Van Don (right), a participant in the coup which overthrew Diem, is garlanded with flowers by jubilant students on 4 November, 1963.

the press; nor was he alone in this. Correspondents such as Malcolm Browne, Neil Sheehan and David Halberstam began to question official MACV optimism; it was the beginning of the credibility gap.

The adverse effects of the Diems' ineptitude and miscalculation did not end with military failure against the Viet Cong. Suspicious of all who did not share their Catholic faith, and having enjoyed success in suppressing the Hoa Hao and Cao Dai, they embarked on an anti-Buddhist campaign. They were egged on by extremist elements within the Buddhist community, perhaps encouraged by communist *agents provocateurs*, but

Buddhist grievances were real enough and the Diems needed little provocation. In May, troops in Hue opened fire on a crowd celebrating the birth of the Buddha, and Army units were shortly raiding pagodas across the country. The response was as dramatic as it was unexpected: on 11 June, 1963, Buddhist monk Quang Duc calmly assumed the lotus position at a busy Saigon intersection, prayed as an assistant poured gasoline over him, and calmly struck a match. His self-immolation before press photographers, who had been tipped off to be present, was the first of several. Madam Nhu's outrageous statements lent dignity to the suicides.

The architects of Kennedy's Vietnam policy: Secretary of Defense Robert S. McNamara (left) and General Maxwell D. Taylor (center) confer with General Paul Harkins, 28 September, 1963.

Newspaper headlines announce the unbelievable: the assassination of President John Kennedy in Dallas, Texas, on 22 November, 1963.

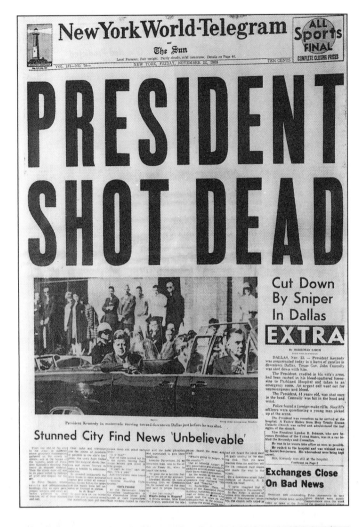

New York World-Telegram
The Sun

PRESIDENT SHOT DEAD

Cut Down By Sniper In Dallas

EXTRA

Stunned City Find News 'Unbelievable'

Exchanges Close On Bad News

The end of a dream: Jacqueline Kennedy, widow of the slain John F. Kennedy, and his brother, Attorney General Robert Kennedy, at the President's burial in Arlington National Cemetery.

With growing religious strife coming on the heels of military embarrassment, it was clear by the summer of 1963 that America's policy in Vietnam was in trouble. In the middle of the cauldron was the new American Ambassador to Saigon, Republican Henry Cabot Lodge. Richard Nixon's vice presidential candidate in the 1960 election, Lodge was named to his post on 27 June. Even as he assumed his duties, U.S. intelligence learned that senior ARVN officers were moving against Diem: these included General Tran Van Don, Chief of the ARVN General Staff, and generals Tran Thien Khiem and Khanh. The question, then, was what to do. Diem was clearly a disaster. President Kennedy's strong public pronouncements against his anti-Buddhist policies had no discernible effect and media commentators were increasingly critical of U.S. support of Diem.

In the event, Diem was overthrown during the night of 1-2 November, 1963, by a military coup. He and his brother Nhu were subsequently murdered by junior officers in the back of an APC near the French Church of St. Francis Xavier in Cholon where they had taken refuge. Diem was replaced by a military government nominally led by General Duong Van Minh. Called "Big" Minh by the Americans to distinguish him from another general of more diminutive stature, he was effective in his dealings with U.S. officials. Unlike many Vietnamese officers he played a good game of tennis – Maxwell Taylor was his occasional partner – and he moved smoothly on the cocktail circuit. Minh, however, was to prove an ineffective leader, and the popular euphoria that greeted Diem's overthrow was ephemeral. Saigon's nightclubs, closed by an unpopular edict of the puritanical Madame Nhu, had reopened, but little else had changed. In the months ahead, Saigon came under a series of revolving-door military regimes as general succeeded general. Minh and his colleagues were to prove incapable of consolidating their power, let alone of governing the country.

The question of the Kennedy Administration's involvement in Diem's overthrow and murder became a political albatross at the time and has never been definitvely resolved. The likely explanation is that while U.S. officials knew of the coup plans and did nothing to stop them – General Harkins was virtually alone in warning that Diem's overthrow was likely to produce even worse chaos – there was only indirect American involvement in Diem's overthrow and none in his murder.

John Kennedy survived Ngo Dinh Diem by barely two weeks, cut down by an assassin's bullets in Dallas, Texas, on 22 November, 1963. He was succeeded by Vice President Lyndon Baines Johnson, who took the oath of allegiance in a nondescript reception lounge at the Dallas airport, his predecessor's blood-spattered widow at his side, before flying back to Washington to pick up the reins of power.

CHAPTER FIVE

PRESIDENT JOHNSON'S WAR

Barry Goldwater's call for decisive military action in Vietnam and Republican efforts to play on his sincerity backfired. His slogan (left) came back as "In your guts, you know he's nuts!"

Right: Lyndon Johnson and summer college government interns, Washington, D.C., 19 August 1964. Sensitive to accusations that he lacked crowd appeal, he frequently addressed friendly audiences.

It would be difficult to imagine two men of equivalent accomplishments and abilities more different in manner, style and temperament than John Kennedy and Lyndon Johnson, the one understated, dynamic and poised – even glamorous – the other blunt in expression, at times to the point of crudeness, and ponderous in manner. A powerful and complex personality, Johnson seemed to some to be consumed by a drive to measure up to his predecessor's image. Highly intelligent, he was acutely conscious of his modest origins in rural Texas and smarted when commentators and columnists drew the inevitable adverse comparisons between his homespun manner and the polish and style of Kennedy's Harvard-educated inner circle. When early attempts to present a polished presidential image met with ridicule, Johnson reacted defensively, retreating into his country-boy persona to a degree which seemed affected even to many who shared his background and accent. Nor could Johnson's considerable abilities be separated from his image; his success in selling his policies and programs to the American people depended on that image, both directly in his ability to project himself in person, particularly on television, and indirectly in his success in dealing with the press. It was in this last area that the

Viet Cong sappers plant mines along a beach. As the U.S. presidential campaign got under way, the military situation in Vietnam was deteriorating.

Above: the destroyer USS Maddox, *on patrol in the South China Sea with the attack carrier USS* Ticonderoga *in December 1964. The destroyer was involved in both Gulf of Tonkin incidents.*

Right: USS Enterprise, *photographed in November 1964. Attacked by critics of the Navy as non cost-effective, attack carriers proved their worth in Vietnam.*

Defense Secretary McNamara explains the PIERCE ARROW raids at a Pentagon press briefing. From the beginning, the Johnson administration emphasized public relations as regarded Vietnam.

An Air Force Cessna 0-1F (left) patrols a rail line looking for signs of ambush and sabotage – the security of lines of communications in South Vietnam was a constant concern.

Right: the photographer's "fisheye" lens emphasizes the excellent visibility from the O-1. Light aircraft were widely used for FAC – forward air control – duties in South Vietnam.

Right: an October 1964 communist-released photo of Australian journalist Wilfred Burchett with Special Forces troopers in Viet Cong captivity. Burchett was involved in exploiting American POWs in both Korea and Vietnam.

Left: the 44th Ranger Battalion in November 1964 after a major engagement near Quang Ngai. The U.S. buildup took time, and in the meantime elite ARVN units such as the 44th carried the load.

contrast with his predecessor cost him most dearly. John Kennedy belonged to the same world as the journalists who covered him; urbane and relaxed, he could joke easily with the press corps, deflecting criticism in a way that that was impossible for his successor. Presidential press conferences were hardly a love feast, but neither were they hostile inquisitions. It was a hard act to follow.

Like John Kennedy before him, Lyndon Johnson inherited a range of problems from his predecessor. Vietnam was far from least among these, but Johnson's main interests lay elsewhere, with the array of social welfare and economic development programs which he was to package as The Great Society. Few historians or analysts today question the importance of legislation sponsored by Johnson in helping to overcome the effects of racial discrimination and economic underdevelopment. But whatever success he enjoyed in the domestic arena was tarnished by failure in foreign policy. As John Kennedy's name came to be associated with a vision of graceful politics, enlightened policies and good government, called Camelot after King Arthur's mythical capital, so Lyndon Johnson's name is inevitably

linked to Vietnam. But to draw the contrast so starkly is not only inaccurate but unfair, for Johnson inherited not only John Kennedy's policies, but also his key subordinates.

When Johnson assumed the mantle of the Presidency, the military situation in Vietnam was deteriorating. Feeding on discontent spawned by the Diem regime's endemic corruption and misguided rural relocation programs, the Viet Cong were expanding their control in the countryside. The first months of the Johnson Presidency saw few major actions, but subtler portents suggested major problems ahead: newer, heavier and more effective weapons were turning up among materiel captured from the Viet Cong, including excellent Chinese-manufactured machine guns and AK-47 assault carbines. Intelligence indicated that North Vietnam's leaders had decided to expand the war, and in mid-March, Secretary of Defense McNamara issued a gloomy memorandum pointing to the seriousness of the situation. At the same time, South Vietnam was spiraling into political chaos as the generals who overthrew Diem proved unable to govern effectively, or even to agree on who among them should try. On 20

Among the first Army soldiers committed to ground combat in Vietnam were paratroopers of the 173rd Airborne Brigade, photographed on 5 May, 1965, shortly after their arrival at Vung Tau.

Secretary of Defense Robert McNamara visiting Vietnam, in July 1965. McNamara mandated managerial methods and the use of quantitative indices, such as the body count, to run the war.

January, 1964, "Big" Minh was ousted by Nguyen Van Khanh, initiating a series of political realignments. Confusion became endemic as political instability and military insecurity fed on one another. In mid-April, the Viet Cong overran the district capital of Kien Long in the Mekong Delta, killing 300 ARVN soldiers, and on 2 May communist frogmen sank the helicopter transport carrier *Card* at her berth in Saigon harbor. On 4 July – American Independence Day – a Viet Cong attack in regimental strength overran Nam Dong Special Forces Camp, killing fifty ARVN soldiers and two American advisors.

Plainly, Johnson had to act, but how? His options were circumscribed politically by the upcoming 1964 presidential election, for the Republicans, in a divisive convention, had nominated Senator Barry Goldwater of Arizona as their candidate. Darling of the party's right wing, Goldwater called for a tough military policy in Vietnam, promising to use everything short of nuclear weapons to win the war quickly and at minimum cost in American lives or to get out of Vietnam altogether. Concerned with selling himself to the electorate and conscious of his vulnerability on Vietnam, Johnson ran on a peace platform, promising to keep America out of war, at the same time successfully portraying Goldwater as a dangerously aggressive saber rattler. The Goldwater slogan, "In your heart, you know he's right!," was turned back on its originators as "In your guts, you know he's nuts!" Still, Johnson was between a rock and a hard place. Determined not to be the President who lost Vietnam, he had to forestall communist victory without appearing as the aggressor – at least until election day. His solution was to bolster the U.S. presence in Vietnam with a discreet increment of air power and an infusion of new leadership. In June, before the Republican convention, he appointed General William Westmoreland, a can-do paratrooper, commander of MACV and named Maxwell Taylor to replace Henry Cabot Lodge as Ambassador. At the same time, Johnson

173rd Airborne troopers on patrol near Vung Tau, 29 May, 1965. The M-79 grenade launcher, held by the soldier at right, proved effective in Vietnam.

A Viet Cong suspect awaits interrogation, May 1967. Viet Cong and PAVN prisoners were frequently a useful source of intelligence, but dependence on ARVN translators posed problems.

Marines flush out a suspected Viet Cong bunker near Qui Nhon on 5 October, 1965. Marine ground combat troops entered Vietnam ahead of the Army, landing near Da Nang on 8 March.

Strategic escalation and tactical escalation went hand in hand: an M-113 APC of the 1st Infantry Division scarred by hits from communist recoilless rifles, 15 November, 1965.

Above: a B-52 taking off from Anderson AFB, Guam, fitted with external bomb racks to increase the conventional bomb load. America's commitment moved up a notch with President Johnson's June 1965 decision to permit B-52 ARC LIGHT strikes in South Vietnam.

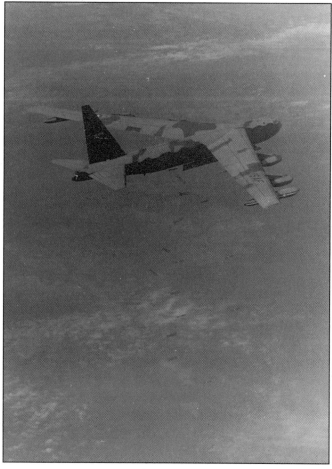

High-flying B-52s could rarely be seen or heard from the ground. The first warning of an ARC LIGHT strike to communist forces in the target area was the sound of exploding bombs.

hoped for a *cause célèbre* that would rally the American people behind a more aggressive policy; he got it on the nights of 2 and 4 August when U.S. Navy destroyers sent into the Gulf of Tonkin to observe coastal shipping and monitor communist radar transmissions came under attack by North Vietnamese torpedo boats, the so-called Gulf of Tonkin incidents.

Later, when public support for Johnson's policies soured, the credibility of the Gulf of Tonkin incidents was challenged, with critics contending that the North Vietnamese attacks were "manufactured" and never happened. With full hindsight, it seems clear that the first attack at least was real, prompted perhaps by understandable confusion between the destroyers' essentially passive intelligence mission and covert OPLAN 34A commando raids on the North Vietnamese coast which were being mounted by other naval forces at the same time. Interestingly, the North Vietnamese were later to celebrate the date of the second incident as "Navy Day", suggesting that a second attack was at least intended. In any case the incidents gave Lyndon Johnson what he had wanted, a point around which to rally public support for a more aggressive policy and bolster Congressional support for an expanded military role in Vietnam. He tested the former immediately, ordering retaliatory air raids on North Vietnamese naval bases from Navy aircraft carriers on 5 August, 1964. The response was lukewarm, but on 10 August Congress endorsed Johnson's actions by passing the Gulf of Tonkin Resolution endorsing "all necessary measures to repel any armed attack" on U.S. forces by an overwhelming margin of 416-0 in the House and 88-2 in the Senate. Senators Ernest Gruening of Alaska and Wayne Morse of Oregon were the only dissenting votes.

Arguments advanced later by retired U.S. Army Lieutenant General Philip Davidson suggest persuasively that even as Congress debated the Gulf of Tonkin Resolution, the North Vietnamese Politburo was deciding to send regular units of the Peoples Army of Vietnam (PAVN) into South Vietnam. Inexorably, America was moving toward a major confrontation in Southeast Asia. In the run-up to the presidential election, both military pressure and political chaos mounted in Vietnam. In late August, General Khanh, unable to govern, dissolved his government and replaced it with a junta composed of himself and generals Khiem and "Big" Minh; the arrangement lasted less than a month before Khanh replaced the junta with a civilian puppet regime. On 11 October, 1964, the Viet Cong attacked in Tay Ninh

The devastating impact of an ARC LIGHT strike, seen from a nearby low-flying aircraft.

A 1st Air Commando Squadron A-1E drops napalm near Ban Me Thuot. Tactical air power weighed into the balance in support of the beleaguered ARVN.

Province north of Saigon in regimental strength, producing heavy government casualties, and on 1 November they mortared Bien Hoa Air Base, killing five Americans and destroying five B-57 bombers.

The 1964 election produced a landslide victory for Lyndon Johnson, but the results were to prove more equivocal than they appeared. Many voted for Johnson because they were convinced that he would keep America out of war. Some, at least, voted for Goldwater because they believed that America was already at war – as indeed she was – and that his promise of swift and decisive action offered the best hope of avoiding embroilment in a long, bitter and indecisive conflict. In the summer of 1965, a saying circulating among officers and NCOs in the first wave of the U.S. military buildup in Southeast Asia neatly captured the irony of the situation: "They told us if we voted for Goldwater, we'd be at war in a year. I did, and I am!"

With a solid victory over Barry Goldwater under his belt, Johnson could face the problems confronting him with renewed strength and confidence. One of his first and most basic decisions was not to sacrifice his social programs for the war; he would pursue both at once: the guns and butter strategy. He was encouraged by the belief that the South Vietnamese insurgency would collapse without North Vietnamese support and by the notion that North Vietnam could be brought into line by measured, incremental applications of military might: the concept of graduated escalation. The first of these beliefs was at best half true. Though in the final analysis the Viet Cong were firmly under North Vietnamese control they had considerable operational and tactical autonomy; more importantly, the situation in South Vietnam had grown so chaotic by the autumn of 1964 that a communist victory without direct North Vietnamese intervention was a very real near-term possibility. The

Air Force technicians work on an AC-47's electrically-driven 7.62 mm minigun, capable of firing 6,000 rounds per minute. One significant innovation of the Vietnam War was the side-firing gunship.

The U.S. buildup in Vietnam quickly elicited protests: picketers were circling the White House a week and a half after the Marines went ashore at Da Nang.

second of these notions, graduated escalation, was a product of the New Frontier, owing more to the theories of business professors and political scientists than to the historical experience of war. Among its adherents was Robert Strange McNamara. Senior military officers instinctively rejected graduated escalation, just as they resisted his notion that the Department of Defense could be managed rationally by the rigorous application of quantitative management techniques. The generals and admirals had a point: war is a terribly inexact business, more subjective than objective and driven by irrational forces not subject to precise control. But they were ineffective in presenting their arguments and, more to the point, McNamara had a good press and the President's ear. Finally, Lyndon Johnson had another significant concern: the possibility that American involvement in Vietnam might prompt communist China to intervene, leading to a wider war. China was in the

Battle-weary Marines near Hoy An, 28 February, 1966. Fatigue was a constant feature of the never-ending search and destroy missions that General Westmoreland's strategy demanded.

The buildup also attracted politicians: Senator Edward M. Kennedy examines a soldier's M-16 rifle in the Central Highlands in October 1965.

Perhaps the tactical feature characteristic of the war: Hueys depositing assault infantry on a contested LZ, in this case near Trung Lap, twenty-five miles north of Saigon, 1 January, 1966.

throes of Mao Tse-tung's Great Leap Forward, but the destructive consequences of Mao's policies were unclear and, in any case, the destruction of the 1937-49 Civil War had not kept China from intervening in Korea.

When Lyndon Johnson determined that America would have to raise her stakes significantly to prevent a communist takeover in South Vietnam, he proceeded reactively and incrementally. In the final months of 1964, the Viet Cong launched a brief campaign of terrorist attacks in Saigon, bombing U.S. officers' billets in the Brink Hotel in Saigon on Christmas Eve. By the year's end, the Viet Cong were mounting attacks in divisional strength and there was evidence that regular PAVN units were operating in the Central Highlands. On 29 December, in a particularly threatening incident, the 9th Viet Cong Division seized the village of Binh Gia within forty miles of Saigon, destroying two elite ARVN battalions; then, rather than fading away into the jungle as in the past, the communists stayed in the village for several days.

When a pre-dawn mortar attack on the American base at Pleiku on 7 February, 1965, killed eight Americans and wounded 106, Lyndon Johnson's patience was at an end. TF-77 (Task Force 77), the Navy attack carrier force in Vietnamese waters, received orders to launch retaliatory strikes against North Vietnam. Under the code name FLAMING DART, the first of these was delivered against barracks and port facilities around Dong Hoi the same day; the second was delivered on 11 February. FLAMING DART was both a prelude to major

American escalation and a foretaste of things to come: the exact targets to be struck, the numbers and types of aircraft to be used, the kinds of ordnance dropped and the precise timing of the attacks were all dictated from Washington. The attacks were launched beneath low-lying monsoon clouds and part of the first had to be aborted because of the weather; the second was timed to coincide with a public statement by the President.

As the FLAMING DART raids were being planned and executed, debate within the Johnson Administration over the nature and scale of the American response in Vietnam was approaching resolution: the national strategy would be guns and butter, the military strategy would combine graduated escalation with a war of attrition against communist forces in the south. Inherent in these complementary strategies was the idea that the internal political impact of the war should – and could – be minimized. There would be no call-up of reserves; instead, draft calls would be increased and the burden of combat would fall mainly on a group with no discernible political constituency, young men lacking occupational or educational draft deferments. In practice, that meant the poor, the patriotic and the poorly educated: categories that were by no means mutually exclusive. Young men from economically depressed rural areas, particularly Appalachia, the deep south and urban ghettos – the latter two with a high black representation – were to sustain a disproportionate share of the casualties. Those casualties were to be higher than they might otherwise have been since reliance on the draft implied one-year

North Vietnamese regulars in training with AK-47 assault rifles and new light machine guns, which used the same ammunition. By 1966 PAVN and Viet Cong forces had standardized on a homogeneous family of small arms.

As America's role in the war increased, so did the importance of helicopters. A Marine CH-46 disembarks Marines, April 1966.

An Army DUSTOFF medical evacuation helicopter moves in to evacuate 1st Air Cavalry Division wounded near Bong Son during Operation MASHER, February 1966.

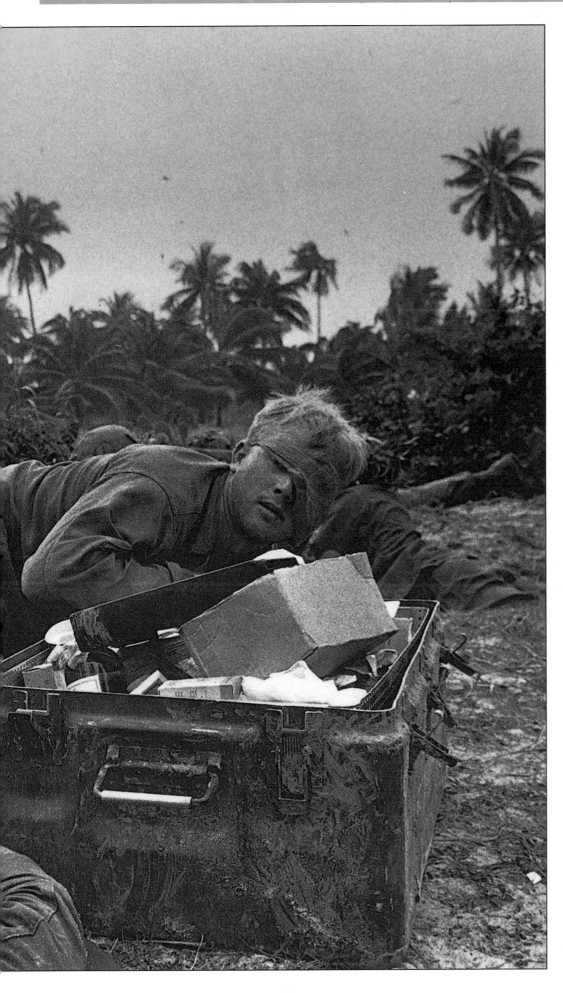

tours of duty, and a soldier requires the better part of a year to acquire basic combat/survival skills in a largely guerrilla war fought in difficult jungle, swamp and mountainous terrain. To Johnson and his advisors, it seemed that the requirements of the war in Vietnam and the war on poverty might even be complementary; by relaxing the physical and mental requirements for military service, hard-core unemployed could be taken off the rolls. Efforts to put this theory into practice wreaked havoc on the lives of the young men involved – called McNamara's 100,000 – and on the organizations to which they were assigned, but the idea that the war in Vietnam and Johnson's domestic agenda could be pursued in tandem died hard.

American combat troops would be sent to prevent the collapse of the ARVN and, if need be, to root out the Viet Cong, but this would take time. In the meantime, a carefully orchestrated air offensive against North Vietnam, ROLLING THUNDER, conducted in part by Air Force fighter bombers sent to Thailand in the wake of the Gulf of Tonkin incidents and held in reserve, would convince the communists that the United States meant business, hopefully leading to prompt negotiations to end the war in the south. ROLLING THUNDER, formally initiated on 5 March, was intended to satisfy no less than five strategic objectives: Secretary of Defense McNamara saw the bombing offensive primarily as an instrument of graduated escalation, an application of force to achieve a negotiated settlement with minimum expenditure of blood and money. General Westmoreland, less sanguine about the prospects for negotiations and responsible for preventing a Viet Cong takeover in the south, saw it as a justification for introducing more U.S. ground troops into South Vietnam; brought in to defend U.S. air bases from mortar and sapper attacks, they could then be used for search and destroy missions while the ARVN concentrated on pacification. National Security Policy Advisor McGeorge Bundy saw the air attacks on North Vietnam as a means of bolstering South Vietnamese resolve, convincing the hard-pressed ARVN that they would not be abandoned. Senior military commanders outside Vietnam, specifically CINCPAC (Commander in Chief Pacific), Admiral U. S. Grant Sharp, and the joint chiefs of staff envisioned ROLLING THUNDER as an air interdiction campaign against communist lines of resupply: an effort to choke off supplies to Viet Cong and PAVN main force units in the south and bring about the collapse of the North Vietnamese transportation system. The tensions between these disparate objectives were never resolved, with consequences for the air war against North Vietnam which are addressed in Chapter 6. More to the point, the Third Marines began landing near Da Nang on 8 March and were shortly providing air-base security. By the end of the month, they were joined by the 1st Marine Air Wing from Okinawa and Japan and by 9th Marine Brigade headquarters. Initially, U.S. authorities observed the fiction that the Marines were present only to provide air-base security, but operational logic quickly won out: to provide security, an infantry force must patrol beyond the perimeter to obtain intelligence and to forestall attack, and once outside the perimeter, it must act aggressively to survive. On 6 April, 1965, President Johnson authorized U.S. ground forces in Vietnam to engage in offensive operations. Whatever doubt might have existed up to this point was dispelled; the United States was at war.

With the advantage of dedicated Navy amphibious transports and logistical support vessels, the Marines were first to deploy, but the Army was not far behind. The 173rd Airborne Brigade, airlifted into Vung Tau and Bien Hoa in May, was the first Army ground combat unit to arrive. It was followed in June by the first contingent provided by an American ally, the 1st Battalion, Royal Australian Regiment. General Westmoreland lost no time putting the new forces to use, mounting a major search and destroy operation – the first of the war – in War Zone D north of Saigon. The arrival of ground combat troops was accompanied by an increase in air strength as Air Force fighter bomber and transport squadrons occupied hurriedly constructed bases. In June President Johnson authorized strikes by B-52 bombers of the Strategic Air Command (SAC) based on

Bien Hoa Air Base, 7 December, 1966. As the U.S. air presence grew, South Vietnam's airfields were filled to capacity.

Guam under the code name ARC LIGHT. Converted from their role as part of SAC's nuclear deterrent force by the provision of conventional bomb shackles and external racks, the B-52s were to play a major role in the war. Arriving silently – they flew at altitudes too high to be seen or heard from the ground under normal circumstances – the B-52s introduced an element of terror into the lives of communist cadres in base areas deep in the jungle. Capable of pinpoint accuracy, the B-52s proved effective in direct support of U.S. and ARVN forces and were to prove a fearsome equalizer in battles to come.

By July, the 1st Infantry and 101st Airborne Divisions had begun to arrive in Vietnam along with a New Zealand artillery battery, and more Marine and Army units were not far behind. The elite 1st Cavalry Division (Airmobile), an experimental organization equipped with its own helicopters for full air mobility, arrived in September and in October another ally weighed in with the arrival of the Republic of Korea (ROK) Capital Division and Marine Brigade. In December, the 25th Division began deploying to Vietnam from Hawaii; others were to follow until, in February of 1967, the Army ran out of deployable divisions and formed the Americal Division from smaller units already in Vietnam. By the end of 1965, much of the force structure which was to fight the American war was in place. The line infantry, artillery and armor battalions

Left: a USAF F-100 over South Vietnam. The debate over the relative merits of land-based tactical air power and aircraft carriers raged unresolved throughout the conflict.

Below: a Navy F-4B, launched from USS Enterprise. When the American buildup got under way, the McDonnell F-4 was widely considered the hottest and most capable U.S. fighter in squadron service.

Army troops, using a smoke grenade, mark their position for a helicopter overhead, August 1965. The drifting smoke indicated wind direction and different colors were used for authentication.

101st Airborne Division troops near An Khe, on 28 February, 1966. Destruction of civilian property in so-called "zippo raids" was a major bone of contention in U.S. media coverage of the war.

were followed by engineering units, logistic support units and communications units; headquarters were formed to coordinate their employment.

In retrospect, it is apparent that the North Vietnamese leadership underestimated the Americans almost as badly as America's leaders had underestimated them, and in November the North Vietnamese challenged the American buildup directly by sending PAVN regular battalions and regiments into combat against their American opposites. The result, in what came to be known as the Battle of the Ia Drang Valley, 14-16 November, 1965, was a major turning point of the war. In a bloody series of ambushes and counter-ambushes in difficult terrain near Plei Me in the Central Highlands, the 1st Air Cavalry Division and supporting air power inflicted severe casualties on the three PAVN regiments sent against it. The air cavalrymen suffered nearly as badly; the 2nd Battalion, 7th Cavalry Regiment – George Armstrong Custer's old outfit overrun at the Little Big Horn – was nearly wiped out. But the North Vietnamese learned that American mobility and firepower could not

be challenged in the open; they pulled back into remote base areas and settled down for the long haul. Westmoreland continued to go after them, sending his units on increasingly arduous search and destroy missions in difficult terrain, rejecting arguments by the Marines that their efforts would be better spent on pacification, winning the hearts and minds of the rural populace and forcing the communist main force battalions to come to them. This established the operational pattern of the war in South Vietnam for the next two years.

In the short term ROLLING THUNDER served its purpose. McGeorge Bundy's hopes, at least, were fulfilled; encouraged by clear evidence of American support, the ARVN began to fight with increasing skill and courage, holding things together until help could arrive. But the improvement was neither immediate nor universal, and the legacy of Diem's corruption and favoritism was still evident. In late May, three ARVN battalions were routed by the Viet Cong in a struggle for the village of Ba Gia near Quang Ngai, recapturing the village only weeks later with massive air support. Nor

Marines take cover during Operation HICKORY, on 20 May, 1967. U.S. troops quickly learned to respect the camouflage and fire discipline of the communist enemy.

Left: Lyndon Johnson's instrument of victory, General William C. Westmoreland, in January 1967. Westmoreland's contribution to U.S. strategy was a preemptive emphasis on search and destroy operations

The end of the war for all too many U.S. servicemen: wounded soldiers are loaded onto a C-141 transport from an Air Force ambulance, Tan Son Nhut Airport, Saigon, 1 November, 1967.

Wounded Marines await evacuation on Hill 861, 29 April, 1967. Helicopter evacuation enabled U.S. wounded to receive quicker and better medical treatment than in any previous conflict.

were persistent ARVN weaknesses the only problem with the American buildup: on 3 August, CBS correspondent Morley Safer accompanied a Marine patrol out of the Da Nang perimeter and observed Marines setting fire to the hamlet of Cam Ne on orders from their officers. The village may well have been Viet Cong controlled and the opposition more serious than Safer knew, but his cameraman's footage, broadcast on the evening news, of Marines setting fire to thatched huts over the weeping protests of old women and children left an image in American minds that was at variance both with the conduct expected of American troops and with what they had been led to believe about the nature of the war. The image proved impossible to eradicate. The credibility gap had achieved a new benchmark, extending beyond the press to the general public.

From the American military viewpoint, the essential structures in place by the end of 1965 remained essentially unaltered for the next two years. Things changed, but – at least in the eyes of those in charge – the changes were quantitative rather than qualitative. The scale of commitment increased from 184,300 American and 22,400 allied troops in South Vietnam at the end of 1965 to 485,600 U.S. troops and 59,300 allied by the end of 1967. During the same period ARVN strength increased from 514,000 to 798,000. At the same time, however, the PAVN presence in the south increased as well and, more to the point, there was no clear evidence that the guerrilla war – the all-important struggle for the hearts and minds of the rural populace – was going well. Debates raged within the American hierarchy over the percentage of villages that had been pacified, the numbers of communist regular soldiers and guerrillas in South Vietnam and the accuracy of body count figures. Secretary of Defense McNamara's penchant for providing support and allocating resources on the basis of hard, statistical data made the debates all the more intense. But in a fundamental sense, they missed the point, for in the final analysis war is more a matter of faith, determination and will than numbers.

One number which *was* important was the count of American KIAs, military personnel killed in action. During the Kennedy years, the numbers were small and represented professional soldiers; from 1966 on, they increasingly represented ordinary citizens: the boy next door or somebody's son down the street. As the scale of operations mounted, so did the numbers. By the end of 1965, the total was 636; by the end of 1967, it had risen to 16,021, and Americans were beginning to ask why. In fact, the communists were being hurt: their casualties far outnumbered those of the U.S. and ARVN, their main force units had been driven deep into base areas along the Laotian and Cambodian borders, far from the centers of population, and by mid-1967 U.S. air power was doing

Right: demonstrators confront military police in front of the Pentagon, on 22 October, 1967. Increased anti-war pressure on the Johnson administration at home matched increased U.S. pressure on communist forces in Vietnam.

The 22 October Pentagon demonstration (below), the largest of the war to date, was an emotional high for anti-war activists.

serious damage to the North Vietnamese transportation net. In May the controversial and dynamic Robert Komer became Westmoreland's Civilian Deputy and brought the myriad civilian assistance and development programs together under the Civil Operations and Revolutionary Development Support Program – CORDS; rural pacification began to make headway. The average combat performance of the ARVN, always good in elite units, was improving; during 1965 General Nguyen Van Thieu and Air Marshall Nguyen Cao Ky, both with solid combat credentials, ousted Nguyen Van Khan from power, ending the chronic instability which followed Diem's overthrow; the Saigon government was proving surprisingly robust, holding inflation effectively in check despite a massive infusion of dollars. But quantitative indices of nation-building and the ghoulish calculus of body count ratios were meaningless abstractions to ordinary Americans. They saw little on their television sets to convince them that the sacrifice was worth the cost and active opposition to the war was growing. On 21 October, some 50,000 anti-war demonstrators ringed

PRESIDENT JOHNSON'S WAR

the Pentagon. The previous week's editorial in *Life* magazine summed up America's frustration:

> The U.S. is in Vietnam for honorable and sensible purposes. What the U.S. has undertaken there is obviously harder, longer, more complicated than the U.S. leadership foresaw … We are trying to defend not a fully born nation but a situation and a people from which an independent nation might emerge. we are also trying to maintain a highly important – but not in the last analysis absolutely imperative – strategic interest of the U.S. and the free world. This is a tough combination to ask young Americans to die for.

Meanwhile, North Vietnam's leaders, in some ways as out of touch with the situation on the ground in the South as their American opposites, had decided that the moment was at hand for the long-awaited General Offensive and National Uprising, an all-out attack by regular Viet Cong and PAVN units which would spark a general uprising against the Saigon regime. It would be timed for Tet, the traditional Vietnamese celebration of the new year, falling at the end of January. In November, as their plans gelled, General Westmoreland embarked on a whirlwind tour of the U.S. to testify before Congress and drum up support for the Johnson Administration. "With 1968," he said, speaking before the National Press Club in Washington, "a new phase is starting … we have reached an important point where the end begins to come into view." In a televised news conference, he used the phrase "light at the end of the tunnel" to describe improved U.S. fortunes, repeating almost word-for-word a prognostication made by French General Henri Navarre in May of 1953.

Military police and U.S. marshalls clash with demonstrators. Although the Pentagon demonstration was generally peaceful, there were lapses and this turmoil was a sign of things to come.

CHAPTER SIX
ROLLING THUNDER
1965-68

On 5 March, 1965, on orders from President Lyndon Johnson, the United States initiated a sustained campaign of aerial bombardment against North Vietnam under the code name ROLLING THUNDER. Less noticed, but of comparable military importance, U.S. air forces immediately thereafter started an air interdiction campaign, under the code names STEEL TIGER and TIGER HOUND, against the Ho Chi Minh Trail, the communist supply lines running from North to South Vietnam through southern Laos. From then until the final withdrawal of U.S. combat forces from Vietnam in 1973, under President Richard Nixon, the use of U.S. air power against North Vietnamese targets was a major aspect of the war. In the event, America's seemingly overwhelming aerial might proved indecisive for reasons which remain as controversial today as was the bombing campaign at the time. Apparently mounted in response to renewed communist provocation – the Viet Cong attack on Pleiku air base on 7 February that had killed eight Americans and wounded 106 – ROLLING THUNDER and, to a lesser extent, the air campaign in Laos were the result of a prolonged debate within the inner circles of the Johnson Administration.

The decision to unleash American air power, a decision urged by the joint chiefs of staff and senior military leaders, had been hotly debated on military as well as political grounds. Some of Johnson's advisors who were the staunchest backers of American commitment to South Vietnam questioned the military efficacy of air attacks on the north and were reluctant to pay the diplomatic price that these would inevitably entail. Others, less willing to pay a heavy price for South Vietnam's independence, saw American air power as a quick and politically inexpensive way out. The military commanders charged with planning and executing the attacks saw the problem from yet another perspective: given the American policy of preserving South Vietnam's independence and presidential willingness to bomb North Vietnam, they looked at the air offensive in classic

military terms: How could air power most effectively influence the outcome of the war in the south? Like many of the President's civilian advisors, they started from the assumption that the war in the south would quickly

A carrier flight deck, photographed in the South China Sea.

Right: sailors aboard the USS Intrepid. Though their duties might seem unspectacular to the uninitiated, the safety of carrier operations is critically dependent on the skill, discipline and training of enlisted deck crew members. Deck crews are divided into specialized sub-units identified by the colour of their sweat shirts. Much of the split-second coordination required of flight deck operations is accomplished using hand signals.

Left: a Republic F-105 in a revetment in Thailand. The big fighter, affectionately called the "Thud," bore the brunt of the Air Force effort against North Vietnam during 1965-68.

The USS Constellation *off the Vietnamese Coast. The limited number of attack carriers meant that each one would make multiple cruises in the Gulf of Tonkin during ROLLING THUNDER.*

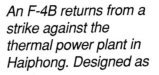

An F-4B returns from a strike against the thermal power plant in Haiphong. Designed as a missile-armed fleet defense interceptor, the original F-4s had no gun armaments.

wither away in the absence of reinforcement and replenishment from the North. They thus envisioned the air campaign as an attack on enemy sources of war materiel and on the lines of supply along which materiel and manpower moved south. To them, ROLLING THUNDER, STEEL TIGER and TIGER HOUND were part and parcel of the same effort. To many of Johnson's senior civilian advisors, however, they were not. To Secretary of Defense McNamara, in particular, the purpose of ROLLING THUNDER was to deliver a message to North Vietnam. By gradually increasing the pressure on the north, the United States would firmly, and in a controlled and precisely graduated manner, make it clear to Ho Chi Minh and his colleagues that a negotiated settlement was preferable to an increase in aerial destruction. At what point that final, decisive increase would come was uncertain, but there could be no doubt that come it would. America's overwhelming might left no doubt on that score. In the meantime, the important thing was to proceed deliberately and non-provocatively, to telegraph to Communist China and the Soviet Union that the United States was in pursuit of a negotiated settlement in the south, and not an overthrow of the regime in the north.

The military leadership strongly disagreed with McNamara's assumptions, believing that his notions of graduated escalation were divorced from reality. They argued that air power should be brought to bear suddenly and in overwhelming force. On one point all parties were

An A-4 Skyhawk awaiting launch from the USS Enterprise on 15 October, 1966. The Douglas A-4 demonstrated an awesome ability to absorb battle damage over North Vietnam.

A long exposure captures the dynamic intensity of the Enterprise's flight deck. Nighttime carrier operations are the most inherently demanding and dangerous activity routinely expected of aviators.

in agreement: once America's full military might was brought to bear, a favorable military decision could not be long in coming. Virtually no one high up in either the Johnson Administration or the military foresaw the possibility of a long and indecisive campaign, the length and indecisiveness of which would be increased by an impressive North Vietnamese air defense system. That system, present only in embryonic form in March of 1965, was to prove impressively capable and resilient. North Vietnam's air defense system was based on batteries of Soviet-supplied anti-aircraft artillery (AAA) ranging from pre-World War II 37 mm cannon to modern, radar-directed 57 mm and 85 mm pieces and even, in the immediate vicinity of Hanoi, massive 130 mm guns. And AAA was only the beginning. As the conflict dragged on, the Soviets supplied North Vietnam with MiG-17 and

MiG-21 fighter aircraft, a sophisticated radar early-warning net and air intercept system and batteries of SA-2 radar-guided surface-to-air missiles (SAMs). The SA-2 had already been used in combat: one had downed Gary Francis Powers' U-2 over the Soviet Union in 1960 and another had accounted for Major Robert Anderson's U-2 during the 1962 Cuban Missile Crisis. But radar-guided SAMs had never before been used in the mass as components of a sophisticated air defense system under attack by a determined and well-armed foe.

The men and machines who would implement ROLLING THUNDER and the interdiction campaign in Laos constituted the most impressive tactical air force the world had seen. Political considerations ruled out the use of Strategic Air Command's bombers, so the burden of the air war against the north would be borne by

A bomb-armed F-4C rolls in near Dien Bien Phu, on 7 February, 1965. Lacking a fighter with comparable capability, the Air Force procured the Navy-designed F-4 in large numbers.

The best training and motivation does not safeguard against accident and misfortune with certainty. Deck crew damage control skill, courage and discipline saved several carriers during the Vietnam War.

America's fighter jocks, Air Force and Navy fighter pilots, navigators and radar intercept officers. Volunteers, they were well trained, confident in their abilities and eager to get into the fray. The attitudes chronicled by novelist Tom Wolfe in *The Right Stuff*, the story of the military test pilots who became America's first astronauts, were much in evidence; laconic and disciplined, their courage tempered with a dash of gallows humor, these men would do it if it could be done. To be sure, there were deficiencies their training – the Air Force had all but eliminated training in air-to-air combat for reasons of safety – but they knew their aircraft and could use them well. For the most part their equipment was up to the task, though there were deficiencies here as well. Engineers had concluded that air-to-air missiles had made World War II dogfights a thing of the past, and of the U.S. fighters in service, only the Navy F-8 Crusader was armed with guns; the months ahead would show the value of those guns… and those of the North Vietnamese MiGs. The principal Air Force fighter to take the war into North Vietnam, the F-105, had been designed to carry a nuclear weapon in an internal bay for use in Europe as a low-level nuclear penetrator, dependent on low altitude and speed to evade radar and SAMs. Lightly armored, however, it would actually have to operate

over North Vietnam, in an intense AAA and small arms environment, carrying large loads of conventional bombs externally. Moreover, the F-105, like most of the aircraft which would bear the brunt of the war "up north" – Air Force and Navy F-4 Phantoms and Navy A-4 Skyhawks – could only bomb accurately by day. The sole exception was the Navy's A-6 carrier attack aircraft, just coming into service; although slow, the A-6 was designed for radar-directed, precision low-level attacks at night. Both Navy and Air Force tactical aircraft were deficient in electronic warfare. Neither service had foreseen that fighters and attack aircraft would routinely penetrate airspace defended by radar-directed AAA and SAMs at medium altitudes, and both radar detection systems to provide warning and jammers to spoof gun-laying and missile radars were still on the drawing board. The Navy had an air-to-surface missile, the Shrike, designed to home in on enemy radars but this had not yet reached the fleet.

The first attacks launched under ROLLING THUNDER were less than overpowering; this was in part because the structure for delivering them in full force was not yet in place, and in part because they were launched in unsettled weather as the dry monsoon gave way to the clouds and rain of the wet, southwest monsoon.

More basically, the political constraints imposed by the strategy of graduated escalation dictated a bomb line that would creep gradually up from the south until the North Vietnamese gave in. However, as the bomb line moved north, the communists showed no inclination to negotiate; instead, the scope and sophistication of North Vietnamese defenses increased. On 4 April, MiG-17s engaged a flight of F-105s that were attacking the Dragon's Jaw bridge near Thanh Hoa and shot down two of their number. The next day, an RF-8 reconnaissance aircraft from *Coral Sea* obtained photographs of a SAM site under construction fifteen miles southeast of Hanoi; it was the first of many such constructions.

Washington's response to the strengthening North Vietnamese defenses was symptomatic of future responses. The President refused to permit attacks on the MiG airfields and rejected impassioned pleas from military commanders to attack the SAM sites before they could become operational; word went out that they were to be struck only if they fired on U.S. aircraft, apparently in vain hopes of a quid pro quo. The first aircraft to be lost

At the start of ROLLING THUNDER, much of the Navy's carrier-based "punch" consisted of piston-engined AD Skyraiders. However, the AD proved too slow for regular exposure over North Vietnam.

Right: F-105s outbound for North Vietnam, March 1967. Designed as a low-altitude nuclear penetrator for use in Europe, the F-105 proved surprisingly tough and effective over North Vietnam.

Unable to see their targets through monsoon clouds, a flight of F-4Cs (below) prepares to release its bombs on orders from a radar-equipped RB-66. Such tactics were only marginally effective.

Smoke rises from a road intersection and bridge complex south of Vinh in North Vietnam after a Navy A-4 strike on 15 May, 1968. Such non-lucrative targets were the bane of U.S. air power.

The North American RA-5C Vigilante reconnaissance aircraft: one of the largest carrier aircraft of its day and exceptionally fast at low altitudes.

to a SAM went down on 24 July, but attacks on the sites were only authorized three days later. The early attacks on SAM sites, tightly controlled from Washington and therefore predictable, produced heavy losses on the American side; these were not just to SAMs, but to the radar-controlled AAA, heavy automatic weapons and small arms which ringed the batteries. Indeed, U.S. aviators quickly learned that they could outmaneuver the missiles – if they could see them in time – and the main effect of the SA-2 was to force attacking aircraft down to medium and low altitudes, where they fell prey to AAA and small arms.

The Air Force and Navy response to the SA-2 was both technological and tactical. The Navy had the Shrike in service by mid-August, but the development of appropriate tactics took time and the first successful attack on a SAM site, by a flight of A-4s led by an A-6, was not until 17 October. The Air Force fitted B-66 bombers with powerful transmitters to jam communist early warning and ground-controlled intercept (GCI) radars and developed jamming pods for fighters which denied range information to SA-2 radars. Next came cockpit-mounted radar warning devices. Finally, the Air Force developed specialized anti-missile hunter-killer aircraft, modified two-seater F-100Fs and later F-105Gs, with an electronic warfare officer (EWO) in the rear seat monitoring an array of radar detection equipment. Called IRON HAND generically and Wild Weasel by the Air Force, hunter-killer flights led by such aircraft successfully limited the SA-2's effectiveness. This success, however, was gained at a price, both in human terms, for IRON HAND duty was dangerous, and economically, for the equipment was expensive. Similarly, the Air Force and Navy put considerable effort into their attempts to shoot down MiGs, eventually achieving respectable kill ratios after a disappointing start. But, as with the SA-2, the main effect of the MiGs was to divert American resources.

The operational results of ROLLING THUNDER reflected the tension that existed between the success of military leaders in persuading President Johnson to permit attacks on targets they considered critical, many of them near Hanoi and Haiphong – power plants, manufacturing and POL (petroleum, oil and lubricants) facilities, railroad lines and key bridges – and the constraining effect of graduated escalation and the periodic bombing halts – there were no less than seven – that Johnson offered the North Vietnamese as an inducement to negotiate. Militarily, the high point of ROLLING THUNDER came in the summer of 1967 when Johnson overrode McNamara's objections and permitted stepped-up attacks in the Hanoi-Haiphong vicinity. On 11 August, F-105s attacked the Paul Doumer bridge crossing the Red River at Hanoi, severing the primary transportation link between Haiphong and the south. When the North Vietnamese returned it to operation in October, it was dropped again. Navy strikes on industrial and transportation targets kept up the pressure. From the vantage point of Washington, the attacks, while tactically successful, served mainly to produce adverse publicity, recalling the previous year's controversy over Harrison Salisbury's *New York Times* dispatches from North Vietnam which had accused the U.S. of deliberately attacking civilian targets thus fueling the protests of an increasingly robust anti-war movement. In fact, ROLLING THUNDER was having a serious effect on the north and John Colvin, British chargé d'affaires in Hanoi, was later to report that the North Vietnamese transportation system and economy was close to systemic collapse.

Whatever the reality, Johnson and his advisors were apparently unaware of the extent of the destruction U.S. air power had wrought. The campaign must be judged a strategic failure overall because, in the final analysis, it had no decisive effect on the war in the south. Moreover, it left numbers of shot-down American aviators in North Vietnamese hands: the largest single body of prisoners of war (POWs); they were to be important pawns in the peace negotiations which ended U.S. military involvement in the war. Military commanders and fighter jocks deeply resented Johnson's and McNamara's tight control of the tactical details of ROLLING THUNDER and, when the President announced the campaign's termination in the wake of the 1968 Tet Offensive, few mourned its passing.

In contrast to ROLLING THUNDER, the air campaign in Laos was driven by a straightforward military objective: to interdict the flow of men and supplies from North to South Vietnam. The effort was therefore relatively unhampered by micro-management from the top, but,

In a reenactment for propaganda cameras, Air Force pilot Lt Hayden Lockhardt is captured by North Vietnamese militia; the photograph was released on 13 March, 1965. Eight years would pass before men such as Lockhardt were released.

on the other hand, it was marked by considerable inter-service wrangling over just who would control what, when and how. At first, TIGER HOUND was controlled by General Westmoreland's staff in Saigon, on the premise that the target area was part of the extended battlefield in South Vietnam, while the Air Force controlled STEEL TIGER and the bulk of the air assets involved. The Air Force objected to this arrangement on the basis that it violated the principle of unity of command and, in 1968, it was given control of the entire air interdiction effort against the Ho Chi Minh Trail and STEEL TIGER absorbed TIGER HOUND. A similar set of relationships

came into play over North Vietnam immediately above the DMZ, which the Marines considered a part of their extended battlefield. The issue in this case was complicated by a sharp philosophical divergence between the Air Force and the Marines, who preferred to give their ground commanders direct control of Marine air. In South Vietnam, the result was an elaborate compromise in which the Marines nominally relinquished control to the Air Force under certain specific circumstances but generally retained first call on Marine aircraft. Called TALLY HO, the area above the DMZ fell under joint Air Force/Marine auspices. Like STEEL

Air Force helicopter units were formed to rescue aviators downed "Up North"; A-1s provided search and fire support. The Sikorsky HH-53 "Super Jolly Green" (top right-hand corner) entered service in 1968.

TIGER, it was exempted from the bombing halt when ROLLING THUNDER was cancelled.

In all these areas, U.S. airmen engaged in a day-in, day-out effort to staunch the southward flow of communist manpower and materiel. Though communist defenses were generally more intense in TALLY HO, particularly when a communist ground offensive was under way, the most bitterly fought campaign was in south Laos where the Air Force pulled out all the stops in an effort to make interdiction work. B-52s were thrown into the struggle, particularly in attacks on staging and storage areas in the Trail's southern termini. Secretary of Defense McNamara also ordered the Trail to be sown with air-dropped seismic detectors and listening devices, monitored from a special, computerized facility at Nakhon Phanom in Thailand, to detect truck and troop movements. The struggle followed an annual rhythm,

with activity slacking off during the wet summer monsoon, then picking up to reach fever intensity between November and May as dry roads permitted trucks to move, and good flying weather helped airmen to locate them. In November of 1968, the 7th Air Force formally recognized the seasonal rhythm of the air war in southern Laos by instituting a series of annual dry monsoon campaigns under the code name COMMANDO HUNT, which continued through to the end of American involvement in the war. SAM coverage rarely intruded into STEEL TIGER, though radar-controlled AAA was common, and the Air Force made extensive use of piston-engined aircraft and multi-engined aircraft, which had less evasive capacity than fighters but a more useful load capacity.

Communist trucks moved along the Ho Chi Minh Trail almost entirely by darkness and holed up in

A pre-WWII vintage North Vietnamese 37 mm anti-aircraft gun. Soviet-supplied SA-2 surface-to-air missiles forced U.S. aircraft down to within range of anti-aircraft artillery and small arms.

A Soviet news agency photograph of a North Vietnamese 12.7 mm anti-aircraft machine gun crew.

camouflaged revetments, caves and bunkers during the day, so that the campaign developed a daily rhythm. By day, jet fighter bombers, guided by forward air controllers (FACs) who were assigned a particular segment of the Trail, attacked road segments, river crossings and suspected storage areas. By night, a small and increasingly specialized armada came out to hunt trucks. Antiquated piston-engined A-26s and T-28s were used for a time, and C-123s and C-130s were used to drop flares for marauding fighter bombers. F-4s, working in pairs and dropping their own flares, were used with some success. It was dangerous work in which vertigo and the karst ridges and mountains of Laos, invisible in the darkness, were as much of a threat as enemy fire.

The side-firing AC-47 gunship, a World War II transport fitted with side-firing electrically-driven machine guns aimed by means of a light-amplifying starlight scope,

had proven highly successful in South Vietnam. These aircraft were sent over the Ho Chi Minh Trail and achieved some initial success, but then suffered heavy losses to radar-controlled AAA and had to be withdrawn in the summer of 1966. The problem was not the concept, but the AC-47's lack of electronic countermeasures and its limited performance and so the Air Force developed an advanced gunship based on the C-130 four-engined turboprop transport. The definitive version of this, the AC-130H, mounting a 105 mm howitzer plus 40 mm and 20 mm cannon, became the bane of truck drivers on the Trail. Fitted with an impressive array of devices for night work, including low-light-level television, infra-red sensors and a device which could detect the electrical emissions of truck spark plugs, the AC-130s achieved an impressive tally of trucks destroyed.

The struggle was a bitter one, with communist road

Indicative of the total mobilization of North Vietnamese resources, an all-female crew mans an anti-aircraft position near Haiphong.

repair crews, truck drivers and anti-aircraft gunners pitted against awesome aerial firepower that was directed by some of the most sophisticated reconnaissance, target-detection and fire-control systems ever seen. The value of air interdiction had long been a point of doctrinal dispute among the U.S. armed services, and its more extreme critics charge that the final outcome of the Vietnam war definitively discredited the concept. A more balanced view points to the enormous commitment made by North Vietnam in resources and manpower –

as many as 10,000 workers died to keep the Ho Chi Minh Trail open – to maintain the flow of supplies south. Vo Nguyen Giap and his colleagues on the PAVN General Staff were thoroughly competent and realistic planners, who would not have made such a commitment had it not been vital. The final argument supporting the importance of the air interdiction effort lies in the ease with which the North Vietnamese built up their logistic stockpiles and troop concentrations for their final, victorious offensive in 1975. The contrast with 1972 is instructive.

A North Vietnamese photograph shows a female factory worker armed with a rifle. Such tactics were surprisingly effective: roughly sixty percent of U.S. aircraft shot down over the North were downed by small arms.

CHAPTER SEVEN
1945-75 THE WAR IN LAOS

Left: French paratroops near Thakek, Laos, in June 1953. Unlike the Americans, the French explicitly recognized the war in Laos as an integral part of a wider Indochina conflict.

Part of a French column from Central Laos which linked up with the Dien Bien Phu garrison,16 February, 1954. Although it was a remarkable feat of endurance, the linkup did not affect the campaign's outcome.

A female volunteer carries a gun as protection against Vietminh invaders near Xieng Khouang in the Plain of Jars, May 1953. Laotians generally considered the Vietminh to be foreign invaders.

In the 1960s, Americans thought of Laos as remote, exotic and far away … if they thought about it at all. By the time U.S. forces were engaged in an overt conflict in Southeast Asia, that conflict was the Vietnam War and it was on Vietnam that American attention was focused. In a sense, that focus was deceptive, for Laos had been involved in the conflict from the beginning and was to remain so to the end; indeed, in a legalistic sense the overthrow of the Vientiane government of Prince Souvanna Phouma by the Pathet Lao in May of 1975 marks the end of the American phase of the Vietnam War. For diplomatic and political reasons the American government concealed the extent of U.S. involvement in Laos, but it was real nonetheless. In terms of dollars spent, effort expended and tons of ordnance dropped, the air interdiction campaign against communist supply lines along the southern Laos Ho Chi Minh Trail was a major campaign, but it was mounted from bases in Thailand and South Vietnam. More to the point, the toll of American casualties along the Ho Chi Minh Trail was relatively small and was incurred almost entirely among professional military aviators, officers and non-commissioned officers, whose families had long anticipated the knock on the door which meant that a loved one was dead or missing and made little fuss when it came. There were Americans on the ground in Laos as well, but the numbers were even smaller and they too were professionals: Special Forces troopers for a time in the early 60s, Air Force Air Commandos, agents of the Central Intelligence Agency (CIA) sent in to organize, train and advise anti-communist guerrillas and selected units of the Royal Lao Army, civilian aviators flying under CIA contract for various companies, notably Air America, the lineal descendant of Claire Chennault's China-based Civil Air Transport whose men had flown over Dien Bien Phu, and representatives of the U.S. Agency for International Development (USAID) and of various non-government humanitarian relief organizations.

The roots of the war in Laos, like that in Vietnam, went back to the Japanese *coup de main* of 9 March, 1945, but had a different twist. Whereas the Vietnamese welcomed the overthrow of the French colonial regime, French rule had lain lightly on Laos. In the royal capital of Luang Prabang, King Sisavang Vong and Crown Prince Souvang Vatthana had responded to Japanese demands that they reject the French protectorate and establish a pro-Japanese government by ordering a national uprising against the Japanese. Nothing came of the uprising, of course – the Lao were notoriously apolitical – and a Japanese battalion reached Luang Prabang on 5 April after forced marches from Vinh and persuaded the King to change his mind.

Laotian recruits do their calisthenics near Pakse, in October 1959. As in Vietnam, the U.S. initially responded to increased communist aggression in Laos by establishing training missions.

Chinese Nationalist troops sent in to receive the Japanese surrender the following autumn dallied in northern Laos – where there were no Japanese – long enough to seize the opium harvest, before moving on. The French reoccupation of Laos was comparatively peaceful and all was relatively quiet until the 1952-53 dry monsoon when the Vietminh offensive into the Tai highlands extended into Laos causing the French high command considerable grief. Luang Prabang nearly fell to an overextended Vietminh column in early May, but a last-ditch French blocking force and the onset of the wet monsoon saved the town for the time being. Up to that point, the war in Laos had been a low priority for both the French and the Vietminh. Militarily the border between Laos and northern Vietnam was a meaningless abstraction and Vietminh cadres had struggled with French advisors and pro-French tribal forces for the control of hearts and minds in the area. In late 1951, the French, belatedly aware of the possibilities of rousing anti-Vietnamese sentiment among tribal groups in the northern highlands, organized the *Groupement de Commandos Mixtes Aéroportés* (Composite Airborne Commando Group), or GCMA. Significantly, the French took this step with the encouragement of the CIA, backed by a small but important unit of American support: two C-47 transports for parachute drops behind enemy lines. Small GCMA teams, volunteers trained in the niceties of guerrilla warfare, were dropped into remote regions to recruit, train and equip anti-communist partisans from among tribal minorities, in particular the Hmong. The GCMA enjoyed considerable success and, even if their efforts in North Vietnam were blotted out by the 1954 Geneva Accords, the partisans in Laos retained their arms and freedom. It was on this fragile base that American advisors began to build when U.S. intervention in Laos became a reality in 1960.

The twists and turns of American policy in Laos, and of the internecine strife between the rightist generals, initially backed by Washington, the neutralists, under paratroop captain Kong Le who overturned the government and only just failed to consolidate his power in Vientiane in 1960, and the centrists, under Prince Souvanna Phouma, are too complex and too far removed from the central realities of the conflict to warrant tracking. Suffice it to say that, after a less than satisfactory flirtation with semi-covert intervention. the Kennedy

An unmarked Air America C-123 transport in maintenance at Nakhon Phanom RTAFB. The political character of the war and the roughness of the terrain placed a premium on air transport.

A neutralist 105 mm howitzer crew in the Muong Huong area in June 1964. From the August 1960 paratroop coup led by Captain Kong Le, neutralist forces were a fact of life until they were destroyed by the communists in 1966-67.

Administration concluded that it could do no better in Laos than sign a diplomatic settlement in Geneva which in theory removed Laos from the conflict and left Souvanna Phouma in power in Vientiane.

In the intervening years, the Pathet Lao, backed by more or less undisguised North Vietnamese military support, became increasingly active in the eastern half of Laos. That they were stopped short of total victory was largely attributable to two individuals, Laotian Army Vang Pao and Edgar "Pop" Buell. Vang Pao, a Hmong chieftain, and the only Hmong to rise to general officer rank, provided military leadership and Buell, an Indiana farmer who came to Laos as an agricultural advisor, organized the logistics and provided a link with the American Embassy in Vientiane. Eventually, the CIA, recognizing a good thing when they saw one, decided to provide the surprisingly effective partisan organization these two had put together on a shoestring with a modicum of support and they convinced the Embassy and Washington to agree to this. The Thais, who had their own strategic concerns and territorial ambitions in Laos, were happy to help. The air base at Udorn in north central Thailand became a beehive of Air America

A Pathet Lao officer briefs his troops near the communist capital of Sam Neua in January 1970. By this time, the Pathet Lao were effectively North Vietnamese surrogates.

An M-79 grenade-
launcher-armed soldier
of the Royal Lao Army
on guard during March
1970. The photo shows
the rough, rolling
character of much of
central Laos: the road is
an anomaly.

activity and the primary base of the tiny Royal Lao Air Force, whose antiquated piston-engined T-28 trainers proved surprisingly effective as ground support aircraft in the jungle-clad karst wildernesses of northern Laos. Elite volunteers from the Thai Border Patrol Police, mostly ethnic Lao so they could blend in with the local populace, were sent to north Laos as advisors to anti-communist partisan bands. Eventually, they were joined by Thai artillerymen and support troops.

By 1963, the Pathet Lao had withered in importance and Hmong guerrillas supplied by the CIA and operating with Air-America-provided logistics were able to challenge the North Vietnamese for control of those portions of northwest Laos that were important to them. Air America U-10 Helio Couriers and Pilatus Porters, single-engined aircraft capable of landing on a postage stamp, supported otherwise isolated outposts with rice and ammunition and shuttled guerrillas from place to place. Larger C-7 Carabous and C-123 transports hauled heavier loads into valley-bottom airstrips. During the wet monsoon, air mobility gave the anti-communist forces the advantage, and they went over to the attack, seizing the strategic *Plaine des Jarres* on an annual basis from 1967. Conversely, during the dry months of the northeast

Pathet Lao soldiers perform for the camera near the North Vietnamese border in Sam Neua Province, spring 1970.

monsoon the North Vietnamese regulars occupied territory more or less at will. However, northern Laos was a sideshow for them, and both sides continued to pursue the war there on a limited basis.

In early 1966, Air Force F-105s were allowed to attack military targets in northern Laos, designated the BARREL ROLL area. A handful of Air Force FACs – volunteers who were required to volunteer without being told what for – based at Air-America-supported bases in Laos directed air support for Van Pao's forces under the RAVEN call sign. Officially, there were no American combatants in Laos – notwithstanding that Thailand-based aircraft could only strike targets in North Vietnam by overflying the country – and they were not allowed to wear insignia of rank on the ground. It was an Alice-in-Wonderland existence, described brilliantly in John Clark Pratt's semi-fictional novel, *The Laotian Fragments*, and it could not last. As the U.S. presence in Vietnam and Thailand grew, the scale and pace of operations

increased. And as the war in Vietnam grew in scope and intensity, Laos was drawn inexorably into the maelstrom. Since the war in Laos did not exist officially and was cheap to wage, at least in dollar terms, it continued according to its own rhythms even after the American withdrawal from Vietnam. Only with the fall of Saigon, and Vietnam, did U.S. support stop, and when it did, it was with traumatic suddenness. Faced with a total cutoff of support and the overwhelming power of the North Vietnamese, the anti-communist position collapsed, with Vang Pao and a handful of supporters fleeing to safety in May of 1975.

Yet the war continued. Hmong refugees coming into Thailand throughout the 1980s confirmed the combat was continuing as North Vietnamese and Laotian forces moved to stamp out the anti-communist resistance, using poison gas and Soviet-developed microtoxins – the so-called Yellow Rain – according to some sources. The struggle continues even today.

Nixon Press Secretary Ron Zeigler briefs media representatives on the status of U.S. casualties in Laos, on 10 March, 1970. Many Americans lost in Laos still remain unaccounted for.

General Creighton Abrams (center) and ARVN Lt Gen Hoang Xuan Lam (in beret) meet to coordinate LAM SON 719, the South Vietnamese incursion into Laos. The operation was a fiasco.

CHAPTER EIGHT
THE TET OFFENSIVE

With full hindsight, it is apparent that the introduction of American ground combat forces into South Vietnam in 1965 prevented the collapse of South Vietnam. When Lyndon Johnson decided to intervene in force, the ARVN, despite increased American logistical and air power support, were reaching the end of their tether. Whether this situation was due mainly to increased communist infiltration and support from the north or to the growing strength and confidence of the indigenous Viet Cong was, and remains, an essentially moot point. In the light of Hanoi's and Washington's policy objectives, it made little difference. The Hanoi regime's determination to unite Vietnam under its aegis and Washington's determination to sustain an independent, non-communist South Vietnam set the two on a collision course. Any illusions that Ho Chi Minh and his colleagues might have entertained that the conflict could be settled in the short term by direct military means were resolved in the Ia Drang valley in November of 1965. Similarly, General Westmoreland was confident in the aftermath of the first, bloody confrontation with the PAVN that U.S. ground combat forces had taken the measure of the communist regulars; he set out to find them and bring them to battle and both sides settled down to a war of attrition.

By the autumn of 1967, certain key senior communist and American military leaders had persuaded themselves that the war of attrition was nearing a climax, though they would have disagreed strongly as to why and with what effect. Perhaps affected by the need to present generally optimistic projections to President Johnson and Secretary of Defense McNamara, and no doubt influenced by his own can-do personality, General Westmoreland became convinced that his search and destroy operations had done serious harm to the North Vietnamese regulars and the Viet Cong. In addition, though pacification was not the highest of his priorities, the consolidation in early May of the whole array of civilian programs under the dynamic and upbeat ambassador, Robert Komer, gave Westmoreland a degree of confidence that the guerrilla

menace was at least being contained. Nor was Westmoreland's optimism without foundation. His operations had, in fact, inflicted considerable damage on the PAVN and the Viet Cong infrastructure in the south. If that damage was being inflicted at a high cost in American lives – 9,377 American servicemen would be killed in action in South Vietnam during 1967, half as many again as in 1966 – Westmoreland could take comfort in the fact that the body count of slain communist troops had mounted even more sharply. In addition, during the summer President Johnson had yielded to the arguments of the joint chiefs of staff and CINCPAC and had significantly relaxed the constraints on the bombing of targets in North Vietnam. Targets of major importance to the southward flow of communist troops and materiel were hit hard and repeatedly, and by autumn attacks on lines of communications in North Vietnam, including a successful raid on the Paul Doumer bridge across the Red River at Hanoi on 25 October, were creating serious bottlenecks in the North Vietnamese transportation net.

There was, in short, evidence that the corner had either been turned, or was about to be. At the same time, opposition to the war back home was mounting. On 21 October, some 50,000 demonstrators marched on the Pentagon – the largest single demonstration to date and the first one to confront the leadership of the nation's military directly. It was in this context that President Johnson called Westmoreland to Washington in November, to testify before Congress and to make a series of public appearances in support of the administration's policies, and it was also in this context that Westmoreland made his optimistic projections. As he spoke, communist preparations for a major offensive in South Vietnam were well advanced. A militant, "southern" faction within the North Vietnamese leadership and committed to pursuing the war in the South aggressively had gained the ascendancy during 1967 and had become convinced that the time was ripe for the

A dead Viet Cong sapper in the U.S. Embassy grounds, Saigon. Such photos stunned Americans who had been led to believe that victory was at hand. An insignificant skirmish militarily, the attack on the embassy on 31 January, 1968, assumed enormous symbolic importance.

South Vietnamese troops mop up after the attack on the U.S. Embassy and nearby Vietnamese government installations.

In the bitter house-to-house fighting in Hue, two Marines cautiously approach a fallen communist soldier whose arms are raised in supplication. The date is 6 February, 1968.

Marines in Hue, 13 February, 1968. Tanks proved extremely useful in the bitter street fighting in Hue. Note the universal wearing of flak vests.

137

long-awaited General Offensive and National Uprising. In charge of planning for the offensive was the victor at Dien Bien Phu, General Vo Nguyen Giap, who, curiously, had favored a more gradual approach to the struggle in the south, an approach emphasizing guerrilla warfare, but who had been overruled in a bitter internal struggle within the party. To sow maximum confusion in the American and ARVN ranks, he timed the offensive to coincide with Tet, the traditional Vietnamese celebration of the Lunar New Year. For the Vietnamese, Tet has a special importance as by far the biggest holiday of the year, a sort of New Year's Eve, Christmas Day and Fourth of July all rolled into one. Traditionally, both sides in the Vietnamese struggle had declared a truce to permit celebration of the Tet holiday; this was to be the case again in 1968. At the same time, Tet also had historical connotations of a more militant nature: the last invading Chinese Army was driven from Vietnam after a surprise attack mounted during Tet by Emperor Nguyen Hue in 1789 caught the garrison of Hanoi in mid-celebration and thus routed it.

The plan which Giap developed for the General Offensive was breathtaking in its audacity. It entailed simultaneous attacks in virtually every city, provincial capital and town of consequence in South Vietnam. Spearheaded by Viet Cong assault troops, the initial attacks would be aimed at garrisons, police headquarters, command posts and radio stations. These initial assaults were expected to trigger the National Uprising, which would be announced in radio broadcasts across the country, for which reason South Vietnamese national radio in Saigon was a critical target. A follow-up wave of North Vietnamese regulars would consolidate the gains and take advantage of the confusion generated by the outbreak of the National Uprising to complete the overthrow of the Americans and the hated puppet regime. To divert American attention – and perhaps gain a major victory – Giap ordered three divisions to move south and lay siege to the isolated Marine base at Khe Sanh in the extreme northwestern corner of the country.

It took time for the assault teams to infiltrate the cities and towns and only the Viet Cong could be used since the PAVN regulars' northern accents would give them away. American and South Vietnamese intelligence learned of an offensive in the making a week or so in advance, but badly underestimated its strength. General Westmoreland cancelled several deployments of U.S. troops and held them in their base areas as a precaution. General Frederick Weyand, commanding Army forces in the Saigon area, put his troops on full alert. In the end, the communists compromised surprise with a series of premature attacks in towns across the center of the country on the night of 29-30 January. It was now clear that a major attack would come the following night. Westmoreland put all American units on full alert and

31 May, 1968: an ARVN tank in the Phu Lam district of Saigon amid the rubble of war during the "Little Tet" offensive.

An ARVN M-41 tank patrols the streets of Cholon on 5 June, 1968. Though less widely publicized in the American media, a second wave of communist attacks on urban areas came in May and June of 1968; these attacks were the so-called "Little Tet."

President Thieu ordered all ARVN soldiers on leave for Tet to return to their units. Even so, when the blow came it was stunning in its power. Across the country, ARVN troops and security forces fought for their lives and U.S. bases were heavily bombarded with rockets and shells.

The communists quickly overran much of Hue and there was chaos in Saigon: a Viet Cong assault group broke into the American Embassy. Another captured the National Radio Station; they carried tapes announcing the National Uprising, but were frustrated by the foresight of an ARVN commander who had arranged for power to the transmitters to be cut remotely. The next day saw scenes of devastation and destruction. In America, citizens who only weeks earlier had been assured that the end was in sight tuned in to the television news to see footage of flaming buildings in Saigon and of Viet Cong and American bodies lying side by side in the embassy courtyard. A television appearance by an obviously shaken Lyndon Johnson did nothing to restore confidence.

Even in the early hours of the offensive, American and ARVN commanders in the field began to sense that an enormous victory was at hand. With their backs to the wall, the ARVN were finally able to reap the benefits of newer American equipment and better training and they fought with skill and determination. For years, U.S. and ARVN forces had tried to flush the Viet Cong out into open battle where superior firepower would tell, and now the communists had done it for them. Losses among local cadres needed to lead the assault teams and guide them to their objectives were severe. The National Uprising never got off the ground and the Viet Cong were effectively finished as a fighting force. At higher levels of command, the message took longer to sink in. With an

Marines take cover behind an M-60 tank on a body-strewn street in Hue as they begin the long, bitter struggle to retake the city. UPI photographer Kyoichi Sawada captured the devastation left by the initial communist onslaught.

3 February, 1968: a Marine M-60 team (left) takes cover in a roadside ditch, behind a bullet-scarred tree.

In the climax of the Allied counterattack, Marines storm the outer wall of the old Imperial Citadel, 1 March, 1968.

unprecedented number of posts and garrisons under heavy attack, it was difficult to believe that victory was at hand; if nothing else, the enemy had convincingly shown that he possessed far deeper reserves of both troops and determination than American analysts had suspected.

Moreover, allied as well as communist casualties increased and the message was grim for a U.S. command structure that was highly sensitive to American losses. In Hue, where a handful of Marines hung on by their toenails during the first critical hours to prevent the entire city from being overrun, the struggle had only just begun. General Westmoreland, while proclaiming the repulse of the communist offensive to be a victory, was soon asking Johnson for an additional 206,000 troops; for many Americans, this was the last straw. The mixed signals which the President's actions conveyed, combined with an increasing cynicism among media reporters and the inability of the Johnson Administration to explain clearly just what it was in Vietnam that

demanded the sacrifice of thousands of American lives, continued to undermine public support for the war. There is no evidence to support the notion that Giap deliberately sacrificed his assault columns to gain favorable American media coverage, but the effect was the same anyway.

In the final analysis, the nerve of America's leaders cracked while Marxist-Leninist revolutionary integrity held. Even before Westmoreland undermined his claims of victory by requesting additional troops, the communist leadership was circulating a brutally frank assessment of the offensive's failure. They had, the assessment admitted, badly misestimated the mood of the people in the South. Far from rising in support of the offensive, they had turned their backs on the communists and in many areas had actually inclined toward the government. The despised ARVN puppet soldiers had not broken; rather they had fought back with determination and skill. Finally, the degree of surprise necessary for military success had not been achieved. Serious losses had

Marine M-79 grenadiers on the streets of Hue, 17 February, 1968. The M-79 proved effective for putting rounds through windows and for flushing snipers from cover with flechette rounds.

Five-minute break, 14 February, 1968. Note the strain on the face of the bespectacled Marine in the center.

16 February, 1968: a wounded Marine under fire has been crudely wrapped in a flak vest for protection, while blood soaks through the bandages on his shoulder.

Communist rockets slam into Marine bunkers at Khe Sanh; such attacks peaked in February, 1968.

Helicopters such as the CH-46 (left) were a major source of replenishment for the Khe Sanh garrison.

As the struggle for Hue ground on, the battle at Khe Sanh intensified. Below: paradropped munitions fall inside the garrison's perimeter, 21 February, 1968.

been incurred in men and materiel, and casualties among southern cadres were particularly serious. The reaction of the communist leadership to this harsh but accurate assessment was swift and effective: where attacking forces had been repelled, they would disengage quickly to minimize losses; where success had been achieved, notably in Hue, the attackers would dig in and force the Americans and puppet soldiers to pay the highest possible price in blood for every position retaken.

That, in fact, is exactly what happened. As the ARVN consolidated their hold in the provincial capitals and towns of the south, the struggle for Hue ground on through February with Marines and ARVN troopers fighting their way into the inner city house by house, block by block. At home, Americans, already shocked by the sight of Viet Cong bodies in the embassy courtyard, were treated to footage of tanks, pulling back through the streets of Hue, loaded with dead and wounded Marines. Militarily, the U.S. and ARVN forces went from victory to victory. By 25 February, the last communist positions in Hue had been overrun. The North Vietnamese pulled back from Khe Sanh in March after suffering heavy losses. Throughout South Vietnam, local officials and commanders gained confidence as it became apparent that the Viet Cong were effectively finished as a fighting force. In America, terminal disillusionment had set in.

As refugees flee embattled Cholon during the follow-on communist attacks in May, 1968, a boy pulls a cart containing other children and also possessions across the Y Bridge.

Right: a close-up of a group of civilian refugees under Marine guard in Hue. Note the elderly woman and the young child with their hands above their heads in surrender. Note, too, the relative absence of males.

Hue, 4 February, 1968: terrified Vietnamese civilians, driven from their homes by the fighting, huddle together under Marine guard.

The citizens of Hue, the South Vietnamese city hardest hit by the Tet Offensive, go about their daily business once more, in an attempt to rebuild their lives.

In Tet's aftermath, armed GIs stroll warily along the streets of Saigon. Viet Cong cadres in and around Saigon were decimated by Tet, and security remained good until the bitter end.

Losers (left): President Lyndon Johnson at a Washington, D.C., press conference on 27 March, 1968, with General Creighton W. Abrams, General Westmoreland's deputy and designated successor.

Winners (below): Pham Van Dong, Le Duan and Ho Chi Minh at Hanoi May Day celebrations in 1968. Though the political impact in the U.S. of their failed Tet Offensive was unintended, they took full advantage of it.

CHAPTER NINE

VIETNAMIZATION

1969-72

The enduring rhythm of the war: children watch M-113 "tracks" of the Americal Division on patrol near Duc Pho, 12 June, 1969.

The 1968 Tet Offensive was a decisive turning point in the public life of the United States of America, and indeed in world history. Largely as a result of its impact, Lyndon Johnson's presidency, which started on a note of cautious optimism, peaked in electoral triumph in the 1964 election, but ended in humiliation barely five years later. Recovering from the immediate shock of Tet,

Johnson stuck to his guns at first, insisting that the American commitment to South Vietnam should not be abandoned. Then, faced with growing skepticism in the inner circles of the Democratic Party and with waves of increasingly harsh media criticism, he capitulated. His decision to name Democratic Party regular Clark Clifford to replace a disillusioned Robert McNamara as Secretary

American President Richard Milhous Nixon and South Vietnamese Vice President Nguyen Cao Ky shaped the final stages of America's involvement in Vietnam.

155

An 11th Armored Cavalry M-113 crew and mascot, photographed near Quan Loi on 17 October, 1969.

Besieged Special Forces camp, Ben Hut, South Vietnam, in June 1969.

of Defense was actually announced before Tet, and was crucial. Clifford, whom Johnson apparently appointed in the hope that the former's legendary political aplomb and legerdemain would produce a way to salvage the latter's policies, proved to be even less attached to them than his predecessor. With a firm grip on the political realities of Washington, if not on those of the war on the ground in Asia, Clifford determined that a strong policy in Vietnam was a loser. His recommendations to scale back the bombing of the North sharply and to seek a diplomatic exit from the conflict weighed heavily on Johnson's mind.

The decisive blow, however, came from an unexpected quarter: the candidacy for the Democratic presidential nomination of Senator Eugene McCarthy of Minnesota, which was announced in late November. A vocal critic of the war, McCarthy was a relative unknown nationally and pundits gave his peace candidacy little chance. Then, in the 12 March New Hampshire primary, he polled forty-two percent of the vote to Johnson's forty-

Montagnards on patrol with U.S. Special Forces. The Allies were willing to accept the human burden of the war, but were only actually able to do so up to a point.

eight percent. For a president in office, this result was an unprecedented rebuke from within his own party. That the exit polls showed that much of McCarthy's support came from "hawks" protesting the President's reluctance to pursue the war more vigorously was irrelevant. With Johnson's vulnerability revealed, Senator Robert Kennedy of New York, younger brother of the martyred President, announced his candidacy only four days later.

A coterie of senior, diplomatically experienced advisors to whom Johnson turned for counsel, the so-called "Wise Old Men", backed Clifford by recommending that America sharply reduce her military commitment to Vietnam. A discouraged and humiliated Johnson appeared on television on 31 March to announce that he would not run for reelection, that he would enter into negotiations with the North Vietnamese and that he had ordered a halt to all bombing of North Vietnam north of 19° latitude. Although formal termination was not until 31 October, the latter in effect cancelled ROLLING THUNDER.

The ensuing contest for the 1968 Democratic presidential nomination was the most divisive national political struggle in recent American history. Torn by loyalty to the President, Vice President Hubert Humphrey did not declare his candidacy for the presidency until 27 April, a candidacy that faced enormous difficulties from the start. Public disorder, of which there was plenty during the spring, summer and fall of 1968, rarely helps an administration in power. Anti-administration demonstrations were becoming increasingly large and noisy, and the assassination of civil rights leader Martin Luther King on 5 April sparked riots in inner-city black

As the American commitment to the war winds down, a trooper of the 11th Armored Cavalry cleans the receiver of his .50 caliber turret gun. The clean-up came during a pause in a road-cutting operation near the Cambodian border on 20 December, 1969.

11th Armored Cavalry APCs formed into a laager for nighttime security near Quan Loi, in October 1969.

A Special Forces-trained montagnard strike force in battle dress, November 1969.

ghettos across the country. Running on a peace platform of his own, Robert Kennedy quickly outdistanced McCarthy only to be struck down by an assassin's bullet on 5 June as his supporters were celebrating a stunning victory in the California primary, which had made him the leading contender. With the advantages of incumbency, Hubert Humphrey won the nomination, but only after a bruising struggle at the National Convention in Chicago. The convention was marked both by disorder on the floor, where news media representatives including CBS television reporter Dan Rather were beaten up by Chicago police, and by violent demonstrations and riots outside the convention hall.

The Republican nomination that year went to Richard Milhous Nixon, who was written off in 1962 by most journalists and political analysts after an immoderate outburst at the media in the wake of his defeat by Pat Brown in the California gubernatorial election. But after licking his wounds, Nixon concluded that there might yet be life after death in politics. While Nelson Rockefeller went home to New York to sulk after Barry Goldwater

Right: Air Force F-4s at work. With greater sensitivity to U.S. casualties in the wake of the Tet offensive in 1968 came increased dependence on air power.

Below: the scene northwest of Dak To in the Central Highlands, near the Cambodian border. Tet may have changed the political landscape, but the geographic and strategic realities of the war remained the same.

Like air power, armored vehicles promised to help reduce American casualties. M-113s (left) were secure against small arms and their heavy .50 caliber top guns provided effective suppressive firepower.

The crew of a Bell AH-1G Huey Cobra confer with their mission commanders before liftoff, July 1970. As ground-troop strength diminished, Army aviators picked up more of the burden of combat.

OH-6A Cayuse light observation helicopters of the 1st Cavalry Division. Used aggressively, they were highly effective in scouting out communist forces.

Too unwieldy for assault operations, the Army Boeing Vertol CH-47, photographed while supporting the Cambodian incursion in June 1970, was highly effective for combat logistic support.

trounced him at the 1964 convention, Nixon supported the ticket and worked hard in the ensuing years for Republican candidates across the country, building up a stock of goodwill among party regulars. Pundits' prognostications to the contrary, the Republican convention wasn't even close; Nixon won handily on the first ballot. Taking full advantage of his opponent's liabilities, Nixon, an aloof personality never noted for personal warmth, won a narrow victory in the November presidential election.

For really heavy loads, the Army procured the Sikorsky CH-54 (below), ideal for transporting a 155 mm howitzer to a hilltop Marine fire base.

The smaller Vertol CH-46 (left) was the standard Marine logistic support helicopter.

Below: Army Medical Corps DUSTOFF Hueys evacuating a wounded soldier from "Hamburger Hill" on 18 May, 1969.

Richard Nixon assumed the Presidency in January of 1969 with a declared Vietnam policy of peace with honor and, so his campaign speeches had advertised, a secret plan to end the war. If the contents of that plan were obscure by definition, certain realities that he faced were abundantly clear. The most basic of these was that the American people would not tolerate a major U.S. presence on the ground in Vietnam for much longer: Lyndon Johnson's agony in the wake of the 1968 Tet Offensive had made that abundantly clear. The second was that the economic consequences – accelerating budget deficits and rising inflation – of Lyndon Johnson's

guns and butter policy would have to be addressed. Judging from his actions, Nixon's plan had three basic elements. Firstly, American ground combat units would be progressively withdrawn from Vietnam and the burden of the ground war turned over to the ARVN who, by way of compensation, would receive an injection of funds and equipment. Termed Vietnamization, this was the hard core of Nixon's policy. Secondly, Nixon intended to pursue negotiations with the communists, both to defuse critics at home in the short term and to secure an end to U.S. military involvement on acceptable terms in the long term. The key to the plan was its third element: the

American withdrawal was to be covered by a series of sharp military escalations. Militarily, these were intended to keep the communists off balance and to give the ARVN experience in large-scale operations. They were also intended as an inducement to the communists to negotiate.

The first and most notorious of these escalations was the May 1970 incursion into Cambodia to clear out communist staging areas and support bases along the border. It had the intended effect of giving ARVN and U.S. forces along the Cambodian border breathing space while the withdrawal proceeded, but inspired a renewed wave of anti-war protests in America, which culminated in the Kent State incident, when Ohio National Guardsmen assailed by rock-throwing demonstrators panicked and opened fire on the crowd, killing four. The second such escalation was an ARVN operation in February 1971 that was intended to cut the Ho Chi Minh Trail at Tchepone by means of a westward drive into Laos from Khe Sanh. Called Lam Son 719, the operation was backed by U.S. fixed-wing air power and helicopters and promised to inflict serious harm on the North Vietnamese. However, in part through the incompetence of the South Vietnamese commander, General Hoang

South Vietnamese Rangers (right) return from a riverine raid along the Mekong near the Cambodian border on 31 March, 1970.

Below: Tuy Hoa Air Base, South Vietnam, September 1970.

Xuan Lam, it turned into a major ARVN setback. Although most units fought well, the North Vietnamese response was swift and effective and the South Vietnamese were soon forced to withdraw with U.S. helicopter losses mounting alarmingly as Army aviators ran up against the AAA defenses of the Ho Chi Minh Trail. The ARVN briefly occupied Tchepone, but the communist lines of communication were never effectively cut and the final stages of the withdrawal approached a rout.

On the whole, however, Vietnamization worked better than the critics – both hawks and doves – had predicted. Forced to assume the burden of their defense, the ARVN showed a marked improvement in combat effectiveness. Elite ARVN units had always been good, but now even ordinary units were showing considerable competence. As the American withdrawal proceeded, the military situation in the south actually improved. This was in large part attributable to political considerations. The bulk of the South Vietnamese populace, who had sat on the fence until 1968, had seen the callous

15 November, 1970: tens of thousands of demonstrators gather in Washington to protest against the Vietnam War.

Women of the International League for Peace and Freedom picket the White House, 30 September, 1969. President Nixon's "secret plan" defused protest activity only briefly.

abandon with which the communist leadership had squandered the lives of southern guerrillas and had now chosen sides. Given a choice, they would prefer the corruption and inefficiency of the Thieu government to the brutality and arbitrary exactions of the communists. Throughout most of the populous regions of South Vietnam, the decimation of Viet Cong cadres in the spring of 1968 had given them that choice.

The withdrawal of American ground combat units came just in time, as incomprehension about the aims of the war effort and disillusionment about the means was taking hold among the young draftees on whom Lyndon Johnson's policies had placed the burden of combat. During 1970, the incidence of fraggings – the assassination of unpopular officers and NCOs using fragmentation grenade – rose sharply from the year before. Racial friction became a major problem, particularly in base camp, and in 1972 the Air Force air passenger terminal at Travis AFB, California, experienced a full-scale race riot. The ultimate

After assembling at the Washington Monument on 15 November, 1969, protesters parade down Pennsylvania Avenue. The motivations and impulses behind the protest movement were many and varied. Note the Viet Cong flag at left and the substitution of hearts for stars on the American flag at right.

President Nixon explains the American invasion of communist sanctuaries inside Cambodia to the press, April 1970. The incursion lent renewed vitality to the protest movement.

An open secret of the peace movement: once the serious business was over, demonstrations could be fun! Youths protesting against the incursion into Cambodia cavort in the Reflecting Pool, 9 May, 1970.

Kent State University, Kent, Ohio, 4 May, 1970: Ohio Army National Guardsmen confront demonstrators before a burned-out ROTC building. What seemed to many students to be a combination of principled courage and legitimate protest was about to become deadly.

Tensions mount and people run for cover as the National Guardsmen try to disperse the crowd (left) at Kent State University with tear-gas grenades. Within minutes – on what impulse and on whose orders, if any, is unclear – the Guardsmen, threatened by a cursing, rock-throwing minority, opened fire, killing four. Below: one of the victims.

U.S. helicopters transport ARVN assault troops into Laos during Operation LAM SON 719. Launched on 8 February, 1971, the operation was intended to cut the Ho Chi Minh Trail by land.

manifestation of the problem came in the aftermath of Tet, on 16 March, 1968, when a platoon of the Americal Division under Lt William L. Calley, Jr., seized the hamlet of My Lai in Quang Ngai Province, rounded up the villagers and shot down as many as 400 in cold blood. Though guerrilla wars are notorious for spawning atrocities and although prisoners were undoubtedly beaten, shot in cold blood or thrown from helicopters on occasion, My Lai was nevertheless an isolated incident. Unlike the execution and burial in mass graves of some 3-5,000 civilians in Hue by communist authorities during the Tet Offensive, My Lai was not a deliberate act of policy. The most shocking aspect of the incident was that no immediate action was taken against Calley and the other perpetrators, though it was common knowledge in the division. When word leaked out a year later, in the form of a letter from a young combat veteran to President Nixon and several Congressmen, a new wave of disillusionment set in which Calley's trial and conviction by court-martial did little to alleviate, for though the division commander was reduced in rank and forced to retire, only one other officer was tried – and he was acquitted.

An ARVN M-113 heads west on Route 9 toward the road junction of Tchepone. LAM SON 719 got off to a good start, but collapsed in the face of heavy communist resistance; assault troops briefly captured Tchepone, but to no avail.

Life *magazine photographer Larry Burrows (right) autographs a sign near the Laotian border. Two days later, the helicopter in which he was riding was shot down inside Laos.*

Indicative of the increased ARVN share of the burden of combat, elite "Black Panther" reconnaissance troops prepare to jump from a UH-1 in the A Shau valley, 25 April, 1971.

An M-113 (left) near Tay Ninh, 30 October, 1971, bears an inscription that bespeaks the crew's disillusionment with the war and their hopes for the future.

A flag emblazoned with the peace symbol (below) flies above a U.S. armored vehicle at the outpost of Lang Vei near the Laotian border, 9 April, 1971.

Instruments of North Vietnamese policy: two young, Chinese PAVN recruits armed with a BK-40 rocket launcher (left) and an AK-47. The photo was found on the body of one of the two, after he had been killed in battle.

The architects of American withdrawal, Richard Nixon and Henry Kissinger. National Security Advisor during Nixon's first term, Kissinger became Secretary of State largely as a result of the Watergate scandal.

By the spring of 1972, it was apparent that Vietnamization was working well enough to give the Nixon Administration breathing space. Negotiations with the North Vietnamese were going nowhere, but the withdrawal of U.S. troops was proceeding on schedule and by March the last ground combat troops were preparing to depart South Vietnam. Considerable numbers of advisors to the ARVN remained, to be sure, as did a substantial air presence in South Vietnam and Thailand, but the weekly toll of American casualties was down sufficiently to take the edge off of anti-war protests. Then, on 30 March, North Vietnamese troops came pouring over the DMZ and across the Laotian border in a military bid to end the war by conventional means that would test both Nixon's political stamina and the viability of his Vietnamization policy.

The communists struck first in the north, shattering the ARVN 3rd Division which was defending the area south of the DMZ. The gravity of the situation was worsened by the incompetence of the ARVN corps commander, Major General Hoang Xuan Lam, architect of the Lam Son 719 disaster. American air power and the staunch combat performance of ARVN Marines, ably supported and in some cases led by their American advisors, slowed the North Vietnamese advance in the critical early days. Massive applications of U.S. air power also helped. Nevertheless, Quang Tri was surrounded and abandoned in panic in late April and the situation was contained only when the elements of the elite ARVN 1st Division and Airborne Division halted the North Vietnamese short of Hue. The tide turned in early May, when President Thieu replaced Lam with Major General Ngo Quang Truong, a competent soldier with an excellent combat record, and by mid-June the ARVN were fighting their way back toward the DMZ.

North Vietnamese attacks in the south and in the Central Highlands were slower in coming, but were none the less dangerous. Loc Ninh, north of Saigon, fell on 7 April and the provincial capital of An Loc to the south was quickly besieged by a powerful force of three divisions. An Loc was only secured after an arduous struggle in which the elite ARVN 81st Airborne Ranger Group was committed. Meanwhile, strong North Vietnamese elements were moving on Kontum in the

A South Vietnamese officer and troops near Quang Tri during the Easter Offensive. The communist invasion found the ARVN stronger and better equipped than in the past.

Above: a Vought A-7 Corsair II on USS Constellation's catapult, with A-6s and a COD (carrier on-board delivery) aircraft in the foreground. When the PAVN attacked, U.S. air power was available in abundance.

2 May, 1972: ARVN troops (right) retreat down Highway One from Quang Tri. Despite the element of almost complete communist surprise which created panic in some units, the ARVN fought well overall.

Quang Tri, 1 May, 1972: under fire, American advisors dash to board an Air Force HH-53 Jolly Green. The fall of Quang Tri proved the high point of PAVN success in the Easter Offensive.

3 April, 1972: fleeing refugees pass an ARVN convoy near Quang Tri, as it speeds north to meet communist forces.

Central Highlands. The storm did not break there until 14 May, but when it did, it came with full fury in the form of tank-led assault columns attacking under heavy artillery barrages which threatened to overrun the town. Thanks to the inspired leadership of the ARVN 23rd Division commmander, Colonel Ly Tong Ba, and the American regional chief, John Paul Vann, who were helped at several crucial points by precisely-delivered B-52 strikes, the communists were stopped. In all three areas, it had been a close thing. U.S. air power had been a major ingredient in the South Vietnamese victory, but it was only that. With few exceptions, the ARVN had fought well and in some cases brilliantly; the North Vietnamese had been repulsed with enormous casualties.

In the meantime, President Nixon, rejecting the counsel of his more cautious advisors, determined to take the war directly to the North Vietnamese with a massive application of air power. Ordering major reinforcements to be flown into South Vietnam and Thailand, Nixon revived ROLLING THUNDER with a vengeance under the code name LINEBACKER, inspired by his fondness for football. Relieved of the operational

micromanagement of the Johnson-McNamara days and helped enormously by the availability of heavy laser- and television-guided bombs, the airmen did immense damage to the North Vietnamese supply net. The precision-guided munitions gave aerial interdiction a whole new dimension; using them, Air Force and Navy airmen took out, in a single raid, targets which had withstood months of costly and ineffectual attacks with "iron bombs," the most notable of these targets being the notorious Dragon's Jaw Bridge at Than Hoa. The interdiction effort was also helped by Nixon's relaxation of targeting restrictions; he ordered the aerial mining of North Vietnam's harbors and coastal waters – a measure the JSC had urged since the beginning of ROLLING THUNDER – and on 15 April he permitted attacks on targets in the immediate vicinity of Hanoi and Haiphong. The military results were impressive, and if LINEBACKER only took effect in the south after the crisis of the Easter Offensive had passed, it did play a major role in the success of the ARVN counteroffensive that followed. Better still, from Nixon's viewpoint, it made the North Vietnamese, with whom Secretary of State Kissinger

A truck hit by a communist rocket burns (above) after an attack on Kontum City airport on 25 April, 1972. PAVN attacks in the Kontum area were among the most threatening of the offensive.

A UH-1B (left) carrying TOW (tube-launched, optically-tracked, wire-guided) anti-tank missiles takes off from Pleiku on 4 May, 1972. Rushed from Germany, TOW-armed helicopters saw their first action in the defense of Kontum.

An F-4 (above) drops napalm on communist positions near Quang Tri, 29 July, 1972. With the communist advance halted by elite ARVN troops, U.S. air power took a heavy toll of the PAVN divisions.

Mopping up: a VNAF A-1 (right) drops napalm in support of ARVN forces north of Saigon on 13 October, 1972. The South Vietnamese flag marks the South Vietnamese position.

had made contact the previous year, more willing to negotiate. On 1 August, the hitherto secret and intermittent negotiations between Kissinger and the North Vietnamese representative, Le Duc Tho, began openly in Paris. It was a good omen for Nixon with the presidential election approaching.

In 1972, the Democratic National Convention voted with its heart and nominated Senator George McGovern of South Dakota, a vocal opponent of the war. Decrying the loss of life in Vietnam, McGovern promised to crawl on his knees to Hanoi, if that was what it took to bring peace, and ran on a platform of immediate withdrawal from Vietnam. His reading of the American electorate was less astute than his reading of the Democratic party and the ultimate result was a triumph for Richard Nixon. Noting the disparity between the enormous size of Nixon's electoral and popular landslide victory and his negative media coverage, political theorists gave new credence to Nixon's talk of a "silent majority" which supported him. There was, however, a small and at first nearly invisible defect in his presidency: on 22 June, five men with ties to Nixon's reelection campaign were caught breaking into the Democratic Party National Committee Headquarters in the Watergate luxury apartment complex in Washington. Nixon denied responsibility, and at first even the media considered the so-called Watergate Caper something of a joke. It was to prove otherwise. Though it took time, the investigative journalism of Bob Woodward and Carl Bernstein of the *Washington Post* and Seymour Hersh of the *New York Times* was to prove beyond any reasonable doubt that the President and his men were behind the break-in. Even then Nixon's position was still tenable, but when Congress sought to investigate, he stonewalled the investigation and attempted to destroy evidence linking him to the affair, committing in the process acts which would lead the House of Representatives to recommend his impeachment. However, as Nixon took office for his second term, all this was far in the future and for the moment his position seemed secure.

The famed Dragon's Jaw bridge at Than Hoa after an attack by Air Force F-4s, using laser-guided bombs, on 19 May, 1972. This attack formed part of President Nixon's unleashing of U.S. air power on communist supply lines.

There was progress in the Paris negotiations as election day approached, and in October Nixon scaled down bombing of the north as a quid pro quo. The negotiations nearly reached a settlement on the basis of a cease-fire – to which President Thieu violently objected – only to break down definitively in December. Secure in the aftermath of his landslide victory over George McGovern, Nixon reacted strongly and on 18 December ordered bombing of the north to be resumed. The resultant campaign, LINEBACKER II, differed from its predecessor in both scale and intensity. Pulling out all the stops, Nixon authorized attacks on targets in the Hanoi-Haiphong vicinity from the outset using B-52s for the purpose for the first time. Though uninspired tactics imposed by Strategic Air Command headquarters in far-away Omaha produced heavy casualties to SAMs on the first three nights, the B-52s wrought immense damage around Hanoi and Haiphong while inflicting remarkably few civilian casualties in the process. At the end of eleven days, the communists were ready to call it quits.

On 8 January, Le Duc Tho and Kissinger returned to Paris and by the 23rd they had reached an agreement.

While Nixon might term the results peace with honor, Kissinger had in fact settled for terms that fell far short of Lyndon Johnson's policy objectives, accepting the presence of substantial North Vietnamese forces in the south and recognizing a Communist Provisional Revolutionary Government (PRG) of South Vietnam. The United States was to provide only logistic support to the ARVN and all but fifty U.S. military personnel were to be withdrawn from South Vietnam. President Thieu, sensing betrayal, was brutally coerced into concurrence, accepting out of necessity Nixon's assurance that he would resume bombing should the communists violate the terms of the accord by reinforcing their units in the south. Hanoi released the American POWs, many of whom had been languishing in North Vietnamese prisons under conditions of terrible deprivation and brutality for seven years or more. To most Americans, their emotion-choked homecoming marked the end of the war.

An American POW in a photograph brought back from Hanoi by folk singer Joan Baez after the LINEBACKER II bombings. Despite communist claims to the contrary, civilian loss of life as a result of these bombings was remarkably light.

American POWs awaiting release from Hanoi's Ly Nam Do Prison, 14 March, 1973. The POW release was virtually the only concession Secretary of State Kissinger extracted from North Vietnam.

14 January, 1973: in the waning days of his presidency, Richard Nixon confers with Secretary of State Kissinger and General Alexander Haig, soon to become White House chief of staff.

CHAPTER ELEVEN
THE FINAL ACT

As the final months of 1974 – the Year of the Tiger in the Chinese astrological calendar – played themselves out, American observers of the situation in Southeast Asia were in general agreement that South Vietnam had shown surprising political and military viability since the U.S. withdrawal. Nguyen Van Thieu's presidency had proven surprisingly tranquil politically, and the ARVN had shown that it could fight it out with the North Vietnamese on even terms. The ARVN counterattack had regained most of the territory lost in the 1972 Easter Offensive prior to the cease-fire, and though powerful PAVN forces remained in the South under the terms of the Paris Accords, the communist forces had limited success in 1973 and the first half of 1974. What remained of the Viet Cong had been destroyed during 1972 and the guerrilla war in the south was effectively over.

But the crucial battle of 1974 for the Republic of Vietnam was not on the ground in Asia, but on the floor of the American Congress. The Watergate affair, the power of the press and his own flawed judgement had finally caught up with Richard Nixon, and on 9 August, facing impeachment proceedings in the House of Representatives, he resigned from office to be replaced by Vice President Gerald Ford; with Nixon went America's commitment to South Vietnam and Nguyen Van Thieu. Disillusioned by the futility of the war and aggressively lobbied by a resurgent anti-war movement, Congress decided to "give peace a chance" and, less than two weeks after Nixon's resignation, it slashed the Administration's request for one billion dollars in military aid for South Vietnam to 700 million dollars and severely cut aid to the faltering Lon Nol regime in Cambodia. Already forced to adopt stringent conservation measures to protect its dwindling stocks of spare parts and munitions and with the availability of U.S. air power to enforce the provisions of the Paris Accords proving problematical, the ARVN faced a well-armed and resupplied foe who could not be long in attacking. Looking ahead to the long-term consequences of the cutback in American aid, the more perceptive U.S. intelligence analysts had come reluctantly to the conclusion that an eventual North Vietnamese victory was more or less inevitable. Nevertheless, the combat performance of the much-maligned ARVN had proven much better than expected and the analysts saw no signs of imminent collapse. Even in the inner circle of the last major American military headquarters in Indochina, the United States Support Activities Group (USSAG) at Nakhon Phanom, in Thailand, the consensus was that the ARVN would no doubt lose ground in 1974, perhaps even permanently losing control of a province or two to the communists, but that they would muddle through for another year, and perhaps longer. Cracks in the ARVN facade were not long in appearing: Phuoc Long Province north of Saigon fell on 6 January after a two week battle for the provincial capital, and ARVN reserves of artillery ammunition, in particular, were thin. But USSAG's primary concern for the moment was Cambodia, where the Khymer Rouge were closing in inexorably on the capital of Phnom Penh.

The USSAG commander, Air Force Lt Gen John J. Burns, was responsible not only for the residual support and advisory functions in Vietnam – a responsibility his headquarters had inherited from USMACV – but also for American air forces in Thailand, which fell under his control as Commander 7th Air Force, giving him the title of COMUSSAG/7AF. Included in those forces were two USAF helicopter squadrons at Nakhon Phanom, the 21st Special Operations Squadron (21st SOS) and the 40th Aerospace Rescue and Recovery Squadron (40th ARRS), which had been retained in Southeast Asia in part to evacuate American personnel and friendly foreign nationals from Phnom Penh should a Khymer Rouge victory become imminent. An evacuation plan had been drawn up, under the code name EAGLE PULL, which envisaged a variety of options, depending on how much warning was given and how many evacuees were anticipated. When the Khymer Rouge dry-season offensive broke on New Year's Day, it quickly became

As Indochina spiraled toward disaster Richard Nixon resigned and was replaced as President by former Republican minority leader of the house, Gerald M. Ford. A good man, Ford faced an impossible task.

Representative Bella Abzug (D-NY) and others talk with Cambodian soldiers at a fire support base at Tuol Kauk, northeast of Phnom Penh in Cambodia. Congress had responded to Ford's desperate plea for funds by dispatching this fact-finding delegation.

apparent that the battered and demoralized Lon Nol forces, operating on a logistical shoestring and hampered by widespread corruption among the officer corps, were nearing the end of their tether. Though the Lon Nol forces were able to contain an initial penetration of the perimeter around Phnom Penh, the Khymer Rouge captured several key positions along the Mekong to the south and began interdicting the river supply convoys from Saigon which were Phnom Penh's primary source of supply. After a series of increasingly bloody attempts to fight the convoys through, the American authorities gave up. The last ship reached Phnom Penh on 23 January and the capital was now totally dependent on resupply by air. Since Congress had forbidden the use of U.S. military personnel in Cambodia, this was carried out by contract carriers, some of them using C-130 transports on loan from the Air Force.

In late February, a small Congressional delegation led by Rep. John Flynt of Georgia visited Saigon at President Ford's request – a request made in the hope

28 April, 1975: as Saigon's final hours approach and bombs strike Tan Son Nhut airport in the first – and only – communist air raid of the war, citizens run in panic.

A flack-vest-wearing Marine struggles to control Vietnamese civilians attempting to board a bus for transport to a designated site for evacuation from Saigon, 29 April, 1975.

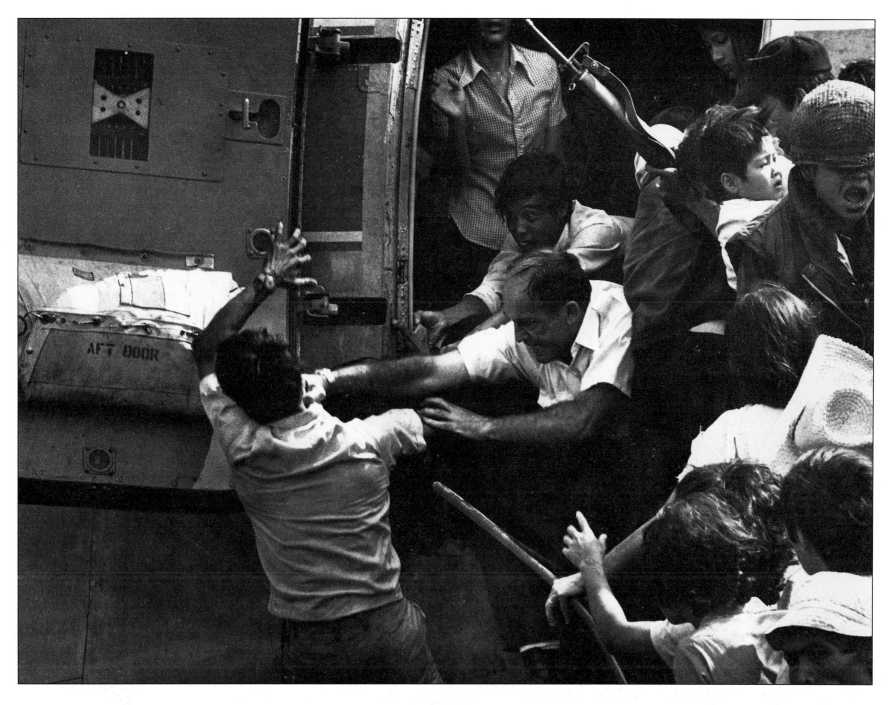

While South Vietnam slides into chaos, an American tries desperately to clear an aircraft for departure as panic-stricken Vietnamese struggle to board a final flight out of Nha Trang, 1 April, 1975.

As smoke pours from a building hit by rocket fire, a woman and children (left) flee.

that the delegation would recommend additional funding for the Thieu and Lon Nol governments. A quick side trip to Phnom Penh left the delegates appalled by the conditions in the refugee camps there – some 2.7 million Cambodians out of a total population of under eight million had taken refuge there to escape the ravages of war and the Khymer Rouge – and they returned with the recommendation that at least some funds for humanitarian aid be restored. Events made their recommendation irrelevant before Congress could act.

In the meantime, the American ambassador, John Gunther Dean, had begun moving non-essential Americans and those Cambodians who might be at risk in the event of a communist takeover out of country. The evacuation at first proceeded via commercial flights

from Pochentong Airport, but then shifted to contract flights. As the ring around Phnom Penh tightened, Dean issued the alert for EAGLE PULL. By the second week of April, as Khymer Rouge rocket attacks threatened to close down Pochentong, a Navy task force was standing by in the Gulf of Siam with two carrier-based Marine helicopter squadrons, HMM 462 and HMM 463, embarked. Dean ordered EAGLE PULL to be executed on 12 April, and at 10:00 hours watched as his security detachment lowered the embassy flag; within minutes he was aboard a Marine CH-53A on a nearby soccer field. Launched with ample warning and controlled by a small Marine command group and an Air Force Combat Control Team flown in by the 40th ARRS from Thailand, EAGLE PULL had gone like clockwork.

A symbol of American failure: evacuees climb up to board an Air America helicopter perched precariously on a Saigon rooftop for transport to staging areas for evacuation, 29 April, 1975.

In the meantime, the situation in South Vietnam had deteriorated dramatically. On 8 January, the North Vietnamese Politburo, satisfied that the initial PAVN probing attacks had stretched the ARVN to the limit, ordered a major offensive. This broke first in the Central Highlands, where the PAVN 316th, 320th and A-10 PAVN Divisions struck at Ban Me Thout in the early morning hours of 10 March. The ARVN 53rd Regiment resisted gallantly, but, being heavily outnumbered and under constant artillery fire, was quickly driven back into an untenably small perimeter. Efforts by the 23rd Division, which controlled ARVN units in the area, to reinforce the position came to nothing and ARVN morale began to crack when the Division Commander took advantage of a slight wound to leave the town. By 18 March, the battle was over and communist units were driving the 23rd's two remaining infantry regiments from the last feasible blocking positions to the east.

At this point, President Thieu made a fateful decision: while the battle for Ban Me Thout was still in progress, he concluded that it was beyond the capabilities of his forces to defend the entire country, but that the southern half, containing the bulk of the population and natural resources, could be held. He therefore ordered the commander of II Corps, Major General Pham Van Phu, to evacuate Pleiku, the regional headquarters and principal ARVN base in the Central Highlands, as a precondition to recapturing Ban Me Thout to the south. PAVN elements had already blocked the main roads between Pleiku and the coast, so General Phu selected Route 7B, a narrow logging road that wound south to Tuy Hoa, for the evacuation. Several bridges on the long-disused road were down, and the relief operation would demand surprise, strong leadership and perfect timing. None of these conditions prevailed.

The first convoys left Pleiku on 16 March and continued to depart unhindered for three days. But no provisions had been made for the civilian populace, and the military convoys were pursued by a panic-stricken civilian mob in vehicles and on foot. Surprised at first, the PAVN reacted quickly and by 18 March portions of the evacuation route were under artillery fire. Worse, necessary bridging material was delayed.and a mass of vehicles and humanity backed up at each river crossing in turn. Panic mounted and observers overhead watched in horror as survivors plodded south suffering terrible heat and thirst. Communist forces finally cut the road just short of Tuy Hoa on 22 March. Desperate attacks by ARVN Rangers eventually reopened the way, and, during the evening of 27 March, the first vehicles began to roll into Tuy Hoa. Of those who started the trek, only a minority completed it. They included some 60,000 civilian refugees, perhaps a third of the total who started, and some 20,000 support troops, only a quarter of those who departed Pleiku. Of the elite Rangers who covered the withdrawal, only 900 out of 7,000 survived. During the ordeal, graphic footage of the "Convoy of Tears," as it was called, was screened on South Vietnamese television, and panic spread to the entire nation.

Meanwhile, as the ARVN scrambled to salvage something from defeat, the situation in the north fell apart. By 19 March, Quang Tri Province had fallen to the communists. Successive attempts to evacuate the ARVN forces of the strategic reserve southward were inadequate and poorly planned and served only to amplify the chaos; Hue fell on 25 March and Da Nang on 30 March. The result was the loss not only of northern South Vietnam, but also of the elite units of the strategic reserve, the 1st Division and the Marine and Airborne Divisions. By 1 April, South Vietnamese forces had abandoned Qui Nhon, Tuy Hoa and Nha Trang and within the week the PAVN was outside the gates of

Refugees board a Marine H-53 in the DAO Compound, Saigon, 29 April, 1975. As night fell, power failed in the compound and panic threatened. Later departures were not so orderly.

A UH-1 is pushed overboard to clear the Midway's flight deck. A final wave of refugees came out in VNAF helicopters to the U.S. Navy flotilla, which was standing off the coast.

Saigon. There, with bitter irony, they were briefly halted at Xuan Loc by the ARVN 18th Division – never considered an elite unit – and the remnants of the 1st Airborne Brigade. Fighting without effective air support – for Soviet-supplied SA-7 shoulder-fired, heat-seeking missiles had neutralized the VNAF's fighter bombers – the 18th slugged it out with no less than three communist divisions for twelve long days before being surrounded and overwhelmed, giving better than they got and dispelling forever the myth of ARVN unwillingness to fight. It was a magnificent but futile effort. By 20 April, only shattered remains stood between the victorious PAVN and Saigon.

Ambassador Graham Martin, a staunch advocate of America's Vietnam policy, had been slow to react to the mounting crisis. Misled by reports from his CIA station chief, Norman Polgar, who had been persuaded by representatives of the Hungarian legation that there were serious prospects for a negotiated peace if President Thieu would resign, Martin refused to face up to the reality of military collapse until the eleventh hour. When President Thieu resigned and departed the country on 22 April, Martin persisted with his inaction to avoid

destabilizing the new government headed by General Duong Van "Big" Minh. Unlike John Dean in Phnom Penh, Martin took no effective measures to get those Vietnamese at risk in the event of a communist takeover out of the country and was slow to order the evacuation of non-essential Americans. It was not until 1 April that the embassy set up an evacuation control center at Tan Son Nhut Airport. There was, in fact, an existing plan called FREQUENT WIND for the evacuation of Saigon by helicopter, but no detailed plans had been made for its implementation. On 3 April, a small military planning group was set up within the Defense Attaché Office (DAO) staff for that purpose. Working desperately against time, the officers of the group were hampered at every turn by the ambassador's lack of a sense of urgency and, paradoxically, by his unwillingness to announce evacuation measures for fear of creating panic. Some of the initial, tentative measures on hand to reduce the number of U.S. citizens and their dependents smacked of Alice in Wonderland; on 16 April, the DAO commander US Army, Major General Homer Smith, encouraged U.S. retired military personnel and contractors to leave the country by cutting off their military post-exchange

The end of South Vietnam: PAVN soldiers in the Presidential Palace, Saigon, on 30 April, 1975. The red and yellow flag of South Vietnam is still displayed behind the presidential desk.

and commissary privileges, as if these would have value in a communist Saigon! A handful of Vietnamese intelligence operatives and their families were quietly flown out of Tan Son Nhut airport aboard so-called "black" flights, but the embassy continued to observe the niceties of South Vietnamese emigration law to the bitter end, and the numbers of refugees remained low. By midnight on 20 April, only some 5,500 evacuees had been flown to safety. At that point the Military Airlift Command increased the number of flights for evacuees, but insisted initially on observing normal regulations, which required each passenger to have a seat and seat belt, so that the number of evacuees moved was still far smaller than it could have been.

It was against this backdrop that the Navy hurriedly assembled a task force with which to effect operation FREQUENT WIND. Clearly, the big H-53s were the best way to move large numbers of people – the DAO planning group had identified some 7,000 candidates for a helicopter evacuation – but HMM 463 had returned to Hawaii and had to be replaced with Air Force H-53s of the 21st SOS and 40th ARRS from Thailand which flew out to the task force on 20 April. The helicopter evacuation was to be commanded by Marine Brigadier General Richard Carey.

Ambassador Martin delayed until, on the morning of 29 April, with catastrophe looming, President Ford and Secretary of State Kissinger ordered him point-blank to implement FREQUENT WIND. The result was chaos. The evacuation was planned to begin before dawn with a series of telephone calls to the evacuees, who were billeted throughout the city, telling them to report to predesignated collection points where they would be picked up by busses and taken to the DAO compound near Tan Son Nhut reaching their destination before the city was awake. In the event, the order was not given until 11:30 and the busses were mobbed as soon as they hit the streets. One of the few convoys that made it had to be diverted to the embassy compound, which was mobbed by terrified Vietnamese trying to get in. Several hours were required for the Marine H-53s to collect the ground security force and refuel, and it was mid-afternoon before the first evacuees began coming out.

Most of those who were evacuated would have been low on any rationally prioritized list of evacuees and many of those who were most at risk were left behind. Though the PAVN SA-2 batteries north and northeast of Tan Son Nhut did not fire, sporadic small arms and automatic weapons fire was directed at the evacuating helicopters through the day and into the night, and numbers of SA-7s were fired at them as well, though providentially without effect. The Marine and Air Force helicopters continued to fly back and forth to the ships standing offshore throughout the night, bringing out over

7,000 evacuees. Having delayed the evacuation, Ambassador Martin refused to depart until all possible evacuees had been brought to safety. At 04:56 hours on the morning of 30 April, in response to a direct order from President Ford, he boarded a Marine CH-46 on the embassy rooftop pad. Though the final Marine guard in the embassy was not brought out until after daylight, America's presence in Vietnam had ended.

The drama had a final, bitter act. When Saigon fell, the Navy of the Republic of Vietnam had not fallen with it. As they watched the ARVN collapse, powerless to intervene, South Vietnamese naval commanders had resolved to salvage what they could. They had brought their vessels into port in the last days of the North Vietnamese offensive to embark their officers and men, and their families, ashore together with anyone else deserving they could cram aboard. As the Bo Doi and party cadres consolidated their hold on Saigon and on the towns and hamlets of the Mekong Delta, some twenty-three vessels of the Navy of the Republic of Vietnam with no less than 18,000 souls aboard stood out to sea under U.S. Navy escort and headed for the Philippines. By 7 May, they were standing off Subic Bay. The Marcos government refused them permission to enter Philippine territorial waters under their own flag, so the armada halted beyond the twelve-mile limit. At 10:00 hours, the command of each vessel was transferred to an American naval officer in a brief formal ceremony; on some vessels the crew sang the South Vietnamese national anthem. It was the end of South Vietnam.

The author of South Vietnam's military collapse: General Vo Nguyen Giap, in a 1977 photograph.

CHAPTER TWELVE
AFTERMATH...

Traces of the American presence remain: the rusting hull of a U.S. tank (above) near Cu Chi, 1985.
Left: boat people, the legacy of defeat and of communist rule in South Vietnam. The numbers who drowned or died of exposure at sea will never be known.

By the end of the first week of May 1975, the last traces of South Vietnamese sovereignty had been erased with the final lowering of the barred crimson and gold ensign of the Republic of Vietnam on vessels of the ARVN Navy standing off Subic Bay in the Philippines. Having brought operation FREQUENT WIND to a successful conclusion, the ships of Task Force 76 and Task Force 77 departed Vietnamese waters, some for long-overdue repairs and maintenance in either the Philippines or Japan and some for the United States. The attack carrier *Coral Sea* was scheduled for a port call in Australia to commemorate the anniversary of the victory over the Japanese Navy in

June 1942 for which she was named. The Air Force helicopters that had participated in the operation had flown off from the *Midway*, standing off the Thai coast on 2 May; now, with a deckload of VNAF helicopters and F-5 fighters loaded at U Taphao, the *Midway* was on her way home. For their part, the helicopters of the 21st SOS and 40th ARRS had returned to Nakhon Phanom, where aircrews reverted to the routine of peacetime training and ground crews worked to catch up with deferred maintenance.

At this point, the unexpected happened. On the afternoon of 12 May, the Khymer Rouge boarded and

199

America's military involvement in Southeast Asia ended with the U.S. response to the seizure of the container ship SS Mayaguez *(left) by forces of the Khymer Rouge government of Cambodia, on 12 May, 1975.*

The Mayaguez*'s crew was thought to be held on a small island called Koh Tang, photographed under fire from USS* Henry B. Wilson *(below), and Marines were sent to seize the island.*

seized the American container ship SS *Mayaguez* in international waters off the Cambodian coast. The Ford Administration's response was swift and decisive. The result was a sharp, forceful action in which U.S. Marines attacked a small island named Koh Tang off the Cambodian coast where the crew was thought, erroneously, to be held; Navy aircraft from the *Coral Sea* mounted retaliatory raids against targets on the Cambodian mainland; Air Force fighters and AC-130s sunk numbers of Khymer gunboats and a marine boarding party from the *Coral Sea*'s escort frigate, the *Harold H. Holt*, recaptured the *Mayaguez*.. The result was a victory for President Ford, but only by a narrow margin. The Khymer Rouge relinquished the vessel's crew, but not before the Marine assault force had become embroiled with a well-armed garrison in a vicious fight for Koh Tang, during which most of the Air Force helicopters were either shot down or so badly shot up that they had to make forced landings on the Thai coast. During the pre-invasion deployment, another Air Force helicopter crashed in Thailand killing the crew of four and nineteen Air Force Security Policemen. The Marines were extricated from their predicament by a combination of hard fighting, good luck, good leadership, determination on the part of the crews of the surviving helicopters, the provident intervention of AC-130 gunships and the sound and timely decisions made at the eleventh hour by an extraordinarily capable Air Force FAC. The arrival of the destroyer *Henry B. Wilson*,

Marines scramble from an Air Force H-53 abandoned on the Thai coast after being badly shot up over Koh Tang; they returned to the island in other helicopters.

Captain Charles Miller of the Mayaguez after his ship's recapture by a Marine boarding party. The Mayaguez Affair ended satisfactorily, but the Koh Tang invasion nearly came to grief.

*Children of mixed
American-Vietnamese
parentage in an
orphanage in Saigon –
renamed Ho Chi Minh
City by its conquerors –
in October 1977.*

whose captain had brought her into the action steaming on all four boilers all the way from a Taiwan liberty port, didn't hurt either: her gunfire helped beat down the Khymer Rouge on the island and it was she who took the crew of the *Mayaguez* aboard. The *Mayaguez* incident marked the last engagement of U.S. combat forces in the Vietnam War. When the last helicopter load of Marines lifted off from the island shortly before 20:00 hours on the evening of 15 May, America's part in the Vietnam War was finally at an end. The last names inscribed in the black marble of the Vietnam War Memorial on the Washington D.C. Mall are those of the men who gave their lives on the beaches of Koh Tang and in the waters offshore and who died in the helicopter crash in the jungles of northern Thailand.

But the war went on. In the aftermath of the communist victory, simmering dissension between the Khymer Rouge and their erstwhile North Vietnamese communist supporters came to a head as centuries of tension between Khymer and Vietnamese nationalism manifested itself. In December of 1978, the Hanoi regime finally responded to repeated and brutal Khymer Rouge guerrilla raids into the Mekong Delta – still home to a substantial Khymer minority a century after Vietnamese conquest in the mid-nineteenth century – by invading Cambodia. In the meantime, the Khymer Rouge, following their own twisted version of the Marxist dialectic, had declared the majority of Cambodians to be class enemies and shot, clubbed, starved and tortured to death far more of their countrymen in three and a half years of "peace" than the Lon Nol Army and B-52 raids combined had accounted for in five years of war. According to conservative estimates, 2.5 million out of some 7.5 million Cambodians died between April 1975 and December 1978 at the hands of the Pol Pot regime's auto-genocidal policies.

One argument used against the American abandonment of Vietnam was the blood-bath theory: the notion that the victorious communists would wreak revenge on their opponents in an orgy of slaughter and reprisals. That argument was ridiculed by peace activists in the final, decisive lobbying of Congress that brought the cutoff of aid, and in a sense they were proved right. The fall of Saigon brought no indiscriminate slaughter, and the imprisonment of hundreds of thousands of former ARVN officers, government officials, anti-communist intellectuals and non-communist political activists was delayed until the international media had been expelled from Saigon. But the flight from Vietnam that had started with FREQUENT WIND continued by sea in small and frequently unsafe and ill-provisioned boats, which were either launched in secrecy or permitted to depart after exorbitant payments had been made in gold to the new government, or to party officials tasting the delights of corruption – it is frequently not entirely

Amerasian children and their mothers on a Ho Chi Minh City street, May 1981. Rejected by their own society, yet rarely allowed to emigrate, most of these children have no knowledge of their fathers.

clear which. The flight accelerated when the Hanoi government expelled tens of thousands of Vietnamese of Chinese origins in the wake of the Chinese attack on North Vietnam that was, in turn, in retaliation for Vietnam's invasion of Cambodia. The flight still continues today. Since the fall of Saigon, over one million Vietnamese have fled the country, refugees who come from every walk of life and every imaginable background from ordinary peasants and fishermen, and their families, to disillusioned former officials of the Revolutionary Provisional Government. Out of the total, over a quarter have died either of drowning, thirst or exposure or at the hands of the pirates who infest the South China Sea and the Gulf of Siam.

In Cambodia as in Laos the war also continues with Lon Nol Army remnants, Sihanoukist partisans and Khymer Rouge guerillas striving to overthrow the Vietnamese-installed government in Phnom Penh, which grows increasingly vulnerable as the PAVN divisions that overthrew the Pol Pot regime withdraw. It is unlikely that this war will end soon.

The problem of children of mixed parentage is not confined to Vietnam: an Amerasian girl (left), abandoned by her mother, begs on a Bangkok corner.

For the few with either money, connections beyond Vietnam, or incredible luck, a new life abroad is possible. Below: Amerasian children departing Ho Chi Minh City for America, 1988.

Smiling PAVN soldiers on a Hanoi street, 1985 – with the passage of time, bitter memories of war fade.

A PAVN unit passes the Ho Chi Minh City reviewing stand during the parade celebrating the tenth anniversary of the fall of Saigon.

Citizens line up to visit Ho Chi Minh's mausoleum in Hanoi. A shrine to the memory of the fallen leader, with his body on display, is a universal feature of the orthodox Marxist-Leninist state.

Khymers wave farewell
to PAVN soldiers in
Stung Treng, Cambodia,
on 4 April, 1985. This
withdrawal was more
symbolic than real, and
Cambodia's agony goes
on with no end in sight.